OLD CITY

OLD
NANJING

Reflections of Scenes
on the Qinhuai River

Text by Ye Zhaoyan

Text by: Ye Zhaoyan
Photos by: China No.2 Archives
Xia Yifan, Guo Jianzhong,
Ji Jun, Cai Yongbo,
Gu Huaming, Zhang Xiuwen
Translatad by: Huang Lin, Hao Wei
English text edited by: Foster Stockwell
Edited by: Lan Peijin

First Edition 2003
Second Printing 2009

Old Nanjing
—Reflections of Scenes on the Qinhuai River

ISBN 978-7-119-03048-7
© Foreign Languages Press
Published by Foreign Languages Press
24 Baiwanzhuang Road, Beijing 100037, China
Home Page: http: //www.flp.com.cn
Email Addresses: info@flp.com.cn
sales@flp.com.cn
Printed in the People's Republic of China

Preface

When he was alive my grandfather often told a story about a friend of his who was a noted scholar. Whenever the scholar went into a bookstore or library, he would shake his head in disappointment, complaining that there were no books appropriate for him to read. Such an attitude was a typical drawback often associated with noted people in society. I have sometimes come across people with the same prejudices. They are not really highbrow scholars. In fact they may not even be mediocre scholars, but they always complain that there are no good books to read. With strong words, they mock bookstores, libraries and all those who write, compile, and edit books.

To be fair, there are books that are not so good but there have never been as many good books as there are today. Book lovers find them with happy surprise in bookstores, on book stands, and in old and new libraries.

In fact they soon discover there are too many good books to read. Books are a part of human civilization, brought forth in a steady stream. New books always come out before the old ones are even forgotten. A friend in the publishing business exclaimed, after returning from a trip abroad, that the number of books in China is simply enormous, especially new editions of old books. To find a good old book abroad is sometimes not easy!

Chinese publishers have a fine tradition: they always try to recommend good books and to urge people to read. As a result, the best old books keep being republished. As a writer I hope I can present readers with a good and interesting book. I often remind myself of the necessity to work hard at my writing.

Over the years I have had the opportunity to come across countless numbers of pictures showing scenes in the history of Nanjing. In looking at these pictures, weighed down by dust accumulated through the years, I have felt the breath and heartbeat of the city's history. I cannot help thinking how wonderful it is to let others look at them also.

This book presents over three hundred such old pictures. Naturally this cannot be a complete collection. History expresses itself in different ways. For people living today, pictures may depict reality but more often than not they reflect something unfamiliar and even strange. In either case they reveal something unique and they all constitute a great charm.

April 1998

CONTENTS

The Sound of Oars and the Shadows of Lanterns on the Qinhuai River

The banks of the Qinhuai River became prosperous as early as the Six Dynasties period from 317 to 589. This picture was taken in 1888.

The Qinhuai is a river richly imbued with culture. At the very mention of its name, people think of its history. Chiefly there are two things they have to say about it. One is its legendary prosperity as many people spent great fortunes here in pursuit of a befuddled life. The other is its sorrow and sadness as, for many, life was too unbearably degrading to recall amidst the singing and dancing that took place in front of the apparent prosperity. When the voices of these two characteristics mingle together, they recount stories of the "eight unique beauties on the Qinhuai," women such as Li Xiangjun and Liu Rushi. People do not want to forget these exceptionally famous prostitutes because they were more patriotic than many men.

Living a loose life yet remaining patriotic! This was a major melody amidst the sound of oars and in the shadows of lanterns on the Qinhuai. It may seem ridiculous, but the literati in China at the time were truly unworthy. After the Qing Dynasty (1644-1911) of the Manchus conquered the Ming (1368-1644), the gentry of Han Chinese origin found it hopeless to attempt to restore their lost dynasty. So they went to the

This picture sheds light on the kind of prosperity written about by earlier writers.

Qinhuai River to express their love for the perished country and found common feelings in the bosom of prostitutes. It was their befuddled life that had led to the fall of the Ming Dynasty and when the country fell, they lived a life all the more befuddled.

When forces of the peasant rebellion known as the Heavenly Peace Kingdom fought their way into Nanjing in 1853, the conquerors made the place their capital. Heavenly King Hong Xiuquan immediately banned prostitution and even went further to interfere in the normal man-woman relations. In his army he had the camps divided into those for men and those for women. Even husbands

The Wenxing Tower on the Qinhuai River in 1910. This was the place where many scholars began on the path to a successful career.

Pingshi Street in the southern part of the city in 1888

The Qinhuai River area before the age of prosperity

The Dazhong Bridge and Tongji Gate. Huang Daozhou, grand scholar of the Ming Dynasty, died here in loyalty to the court he served. South from this position, the green river and long embankment provided a good place to take a cruise on the river.

This sluice gate on the Qinhuai River west of the Tongji Gate had three levels to control the water height on the river.

This inconspicuous building was the residence of Zheng Banqiao, a Qing Dynasty scholar and official. It was a place where the "eight famous women on the Qinhuai" used to perform.

and wives did not have the freedom to do what they wished to do between themselves. Deprived of their way of making a living, the prostitutes fled to the foreign concessions in Shanghai. With their flight came a depression of commerce in Nanjing. The society may have been purified, but prosperity along the Qinhua River no longer existed.

A picture of Zeng Guofan, a general of the Qing army. The photographer is unknown.

Zeng Guofan (1811-72), the viceroy appointed by the Qing court, led his Hunan army to fight all the way into Nanjing in 1864. He knew how to quickly bring back the former prosperity. The easiest and quickest way was to allow the brothels to reopen. Zeng was regarded as "a perfect person" of feudal society and was even given a posthumous honorary title of Duke Zeng Wenzheng. *The Family Letters of Duke Zeng Wenzheng* remains a popular book even to this day. According to the historical records that dealt with the reopening of brothels in Nanjing: "All of a sudden, ladies were heard laughing cheerfully. Businessmen and merchants gathered. By the riverside houses where bushes had grown, white boat windows with red curtains flourished. Men who had been

A tablet praising Zeng Guofen, a gift given to him by the emperor.

staying at home swarmed over. There seemed a great prosperity of prostitution."

Indeed, the reopening produced instant results. In discussing the contemporary economic history of Shanghai, one thing that cannot be avoided is the fact that revolution of the Heavenly Peace Kingdom scared the rich and wealthy in Nanjing so that they fled into the foreign concessions of Shanghai.

Actually the "prosperity of prostitution" was an absurdity. For years the banning and permission of prostitution constituted an eternal topic on the Qinhuai River. Because there had been orders to ban it, there was then the matter of permission, which heralded another round of banning. Going through the thick stack of historical records one gets the impression that there never was a government that gave open praise for prostitutes. In 600 BC, Guan Zhong of the State of Qi had a brothel opened so as to "levy a tax on the evening business and thus enrich the state treasury." This was the first mention of a brothel that is found in the historical records of the world. Compared with this, the state-owned brothels in ancient Athens will have to be content with being the second earliest.

In ancient China, prostitutes were often referred

The Pavilion of Zeng Guofan on Mochou Lake

to as official or palace slaves. During the reign of Emperor Wu of the Han Dynasty (140-87 BC), prostitutes were introduced into the army barracks to "devote their bodies by living in the army camps." Thus prostitutes became means by which the sovereign ruler rewarded and controlled his troops. In people's minds, prostitution has never been something good. Apart from the Tang Dynasty (618-907), almost all the ruling courts through the various dynasties took the position of

This painting of the Qinhuai River done in late Qing times will be more meaningful if viewed together with a poem by Zeng Guofan in which he described both men of position and pleasure women enjoying their life together. He also described the fact that what once were arms for battle were now sold as farming tools and former gunboats served as pleasure boats.

A singing woman on the Qinhuai River

banning prostitution. Such banning, of course, only meant that government officials could not visit the brothels. In feudal society prostitution was an official form of conduct, managed and protected by the state which also charged taxes. Not only was it illegal for officials to exploit prostitutes, it was also against the law for women to engage in prostitution. To force law-abiding women into prostitution was considered a great crime.

In ancient times, prostitutes not only sold their bodies but also their artistic skills. In a certain sense, official and army prostitutes were also members constituting state art troupes. And men normally obtained more spiritual pleasure rather than bodily joy by associating with prostitutes. The most prominent difference between the banning of prostitution during the periods of offi-

Gongyuan was where imperial exams for selecting officials were held during the dynastic period. The Flying Rainbow Bridge, in the courtyard, spans a rectangular pool.

cial and private brothels was that the former banned government officials from visiting them while the latter banned the private selling of women's bodies. Put simply, the prosperity of the Qinhuai River had a great deal to do with the existence of officially sanctioned prostitution there. When ancient people wanted to seek romantic pleasures, they could come there with their money. In ancient times, there were specifics about where a brothel could operate. Thanks to its privilege of being the venue for brothels, the Qinhuai River area also had the opportunity for economic growth.

The Sequal to the Notes of Banqiao published during the reign of Emperor Qianlong (1736-95) records: "Houses on the banks of the Qinhuai River had always been occupied by prostitutes. There were not many such houses, and those that hosted banquets for visitors also used to be quite few. Now just more than a decade later, every house has prostitutes and every family offers women of pleasure. Every day, they entertain visitors of wealth and position."

As official prostitution was gradually replaced by private prostitution, great changes took place along the Qinhuai River. The once revered art among the prostitutes of singing and dancing, and the skills of playing musical instruments and being well-versed in calligraphy and painting, were taken over by the pure transaction of bodily services. Prostitutes had become nothing but tools for releasing men's lust and the targets of exploitation. The river could no longer produce well-cultured women such as Li Xiangjun and Liu Rushi. In the late Qing period, social norms deteriorated and private prostitutes outside the state system appeared in large numbers and spared no efforts in hunting their clients. The domination of prostitution enjoyed by the Qinhuai River was gone forever. The foreign concessions in Shanghai, the Bada Lane in Beijing, Chentang,

Outside the Tongji Gate, the Nine-dragon Bridge built during the Ming Dynasty had five arches.

and Dongdi in Guangzhou soon became centers of prostitution.

In 1923, the 23-year-old Zhu Ziqing went on a tour of the Qinhuai River with his friend Yu Pingbo, who was two years younger. Based on their experience each wrote an essay with the same title "The Sound of Boat Oars and the Shadows of Lanterns on the Qinhuai River". Their writings were published in the *East Magazine*. The essays were regarded successful examples of good writing, thanks to their portrayal of the scenery on the river.

On the northern bank of the river stood the Confucius Temple built in 1034. Local residents in Nanjing referred to it as Fuzi Miao (Confucius Temple), and this later was used as the name for the entire vicinity. The temple was not only where people held memorial services in memory of Confucius, but also the venue for the imperial college. The east wing of the

Ditches cut deep into the stone of this water well prove what the word "time" means.

temple was con-
structed in the 12th
century. From its
completion to the
19th century, it was
where the imperial ex-
ams were held. As a
result, many scholars
could be seen around
the area. During the
exams, students from
south China prov-
inces and often else-

where from the entire country gathered here, adding a
strong scholarly touch to the debauchery and decadence of the place.

People who came to prepare and take the exams
inevitably went to kill time on the painted pleasure
boats, and to drink, compose poems and watch stage
performances. This practice gave rise to many stories
about love between scholars and prostitutes, which
became source material for novelists and the topic of
gossip among the local residents.

Military officials of
the Qing army who
frequented the
prostitutes on the
Qinhuai River. No
wonder the country fell
in their hands.

Upon
learning that
singing women
were banned
from doing
what they once
did at the
Qinhuai River,
Zhu Ziqing,
when he visited
the place for

The Revolution of
1911 overthrew the rule
of the Qing Dynasty.
This picture showing the
celebration of the one-
year anniversary of the
revolution was taken at
the Confucius Temple.

the second time, was gripped by a sense of loss. Apparently he loved singing.

While taking a cruise on the river, he unexpectedly discovered that singing women still went about conducting their profession in a more open and elaborate way. Some of them even jumped onto his boat, stubbornly insisting that people ask them to sing for a price. It is not hard to imagine that the heart of Mr. Zhu, which a little earlier was filled with regret, must now have been beating exceptionally rapidly. Amidst the sound of oars brushing against the water and in

Zhu Ziqing around the time he wrote "The Sound of Boat Oars and Shadows of Lanterns on the Qinhuai River"

the shadows of lanterns, Mr. Zhu feigned a bold smile at the singing women, turned a few pages of their songbook and hurriedly returned it to them. The women then tried to push the songbook into the hands of Mr. Yu Pingbo who did not

A small park by the Qinhuai River in the 1920s

have the courage to take it. All he managed to do was to wave his hand, stuttering: "No, no, not me."

There were simply too many women who came to nag the visitors. This coupled with the attack by pimps compelled the two bookworms to flee in great embarrassment. Later on they discussed how they should have rejected the women properly. Zhu said in a serious tone that to say no directly to them was too harsh, hurting the pride of the women. As for to the pimps, the proper way to deal with them should have been by reason and persuasion. They should have told them, "You are probably not aware that we do not do this kind of thing."

In their essays under the title of "The Sound of Boat Oars and the Shadows of Lanterns on the Qinhuai River", the writers introduced to us how "prosperous" prostitution was at the time. More importantly, however, they also shed light on how different the new generation of intellectuals such as they were in heart and mind from those of the old literati. Mr. Zhu openly admitted his wish to listen to the singing women, but did not want their bodies, just like some of the singing women who sold their artistic skills but not their bodies. The songs sung on the river were all folk songs with melodious tunes that were pleasant to the ear. And they were to be appreciated somberly as songs. Mr. Zhu was aware that singing was a natural expression of one's sentiments. But since the singing women were forced into singing, their songs had lost artistic quality. As a result, the women should be sympathized with rather then laughed at, because of their unfortunate position. Mr. Yu wrote a poem to express his feelings: "I love children because I have mine, I love women because I love my wife."

Their essays beautified the river, misleading readers into thinking that the river water must be clear. In fact, that was by no means the case. The river water became stinking in the 1920s and 1930s. As the culture on the river had changed color, so did the water.

The Number One Park of Nanjing, formerly Xiushan Park, houses a hall in memory of revolutionary martyrs.

The Egret Islet on the southern bank of the Qinhuai

The Confucius Temple in the 1920s

After the Kuomintang (Nationalists) chose Nanjing as their seat of government, the newly appointed mayor, Liu Jiwen, banned prostitution in the hope of giving the capital a new image. Before long, Chiang Kai-shek proposed his new life movement. Ten big characters meaning "Leading a new life and strictly banning opium smoking, gambling, and prostitution" appeared on the walls, injecting people with hope. Unfortunately, the Chinese economy also suffered severely because of the world economic recession from 1929 to 1934. Struggling to get out of the economic pressure, industrial and commercial organizations suggested that the government lift the ban. Dramatically, a heated debate took place over whether or not to ban prostitution on the Qinhuai River. The final consensus was to ban open prostitution. The result, however, was that the number of secret prostitutes remained the same.

Painted pleasure boats near the Confucius Temple in the early 20th century

Peepshow aimed at
attracting children

A breathtaking show
of acrobatics in the street
by the Confucius Temple

A puppet show
performed by two people

Peddlers outside the Confucius Temple

A ceremony marking the establishment of the Nationalist government on April 18, 1927. On this day the city of Nanjing became capital of the country until 1949.

What was reduced was the income in the form of taxation from prostitution that had been an important channel of government revenue.

Despite protests from many women representatives, the once solemn ban on prostitution in Nanjing produced no real results. "New life" soon was dubbed "sex life" and the banning of prostitution became a game that "could not be banned in reality but was only banned in form." *The Great Xia Evening Standard* offered an in-depth report on the issue, claiming that

In the front row are Chiang Kai-shek, Hu Hanmin, Cai Yuanpei, and Wu Zhihui at a ceremony marking the establishment of the Nationalist government in Nanjing.

on Shifu Road, "private group prostitution was in action." In conclusion, the report said: "We stand for the banning of prostitution, but are not against lifting the ban. The most important thing is that a policy should be implemented honestly. What we cannot accept is doing something under the disguise of something else."

After trains were introduced into the city of Nanjing, there was a railroad bridge that stood quite low over the river. As a result of this, coupled with the worsening pollution in the river, the singing and dancing women moved away from the banks of the river to perform in "singing and tea houses" along Gongyuan Street. The painted pleasure boats on the river thus lost their former attraction.

The area around the Confucius Temple gradually became a ground of recreation in Nanjing, where one

A meeting to ban opium smoking, gambling, and prostitution in 1935

had the choice of varied forms of art performances ranging from Peking opera, new style dramas, Hollywood movies, and story-telling with or without the accompaniment of musical instruments. Unlike areas where prostitutes flocked in other cities, it had always been the case along the Qinhuai River that no matter how many prostitutes there were or where they were found, the greatest attraction was always the artistic recreation.

Deep in the minds of Nanjing

The person in a kneeling position at a meeting to eradicate opium smoking, gambling, and prostitution was a chain opium smoker.

The Mingyuan Tower built during the reign of Emperor Yongle (1403-24) was the office of the city government. Since it was located near the Confucius Temple, the great number of prostitutes operating nearby was a great disgrace to the city government.

residents was the doubt that the singing and dancing women along the Qinhuai River only sold their artistic skills, not their bodies. Legacies of the true qualities of the "eight famous women on the Qinhuai," however, could be seen from the behavior of some of the singing women. When the noted novelist Zhang Henshui lived in Nanjing, he managed to bring together a group of reporters and writers with the singing women they knew. At tea parties, the women told their stories and condemned men because of their evil conduct. All the stories later showed up in Zhang's novels. Like the "eight famous women on the Qinhuai," singing women had always been important figures in novels. In fact there were many cases in which singing women eventually became famous actresses. Wang Yurong, for example, later became a well-established Peking opera singer. Wang Xichun went into the movie industry, emerging as a famous actress in Shanghai. The number one lead in Huangmei opera, Yan Fengying, also used to sing and dance along the Qinhuai River.

For many singing women, it was only out of helplessness that they became what they were, but they could retain their clean characters in the world of debauchery and decadence. Many of them tried to take the future into their own hands by working hard to improve their conditions. Wang Yurong won the title of "queen of singing" when she captured most of the votes in a singing contest that displayed her singing skills, but at the same time she secretly learned to read and write at Jinghua Secondary School. Some one tattled on her to the schoolmaster who himself often visited the singing women. The sanctimonious schoolmaster flew into a rage and expelled her on the grounds that her presence undermined the values of the school. Many people found unacceptable a situation in which the schoolmaster could visit

Zhong San, a singing woman performing in the open air

Painted pleasure boats on the Qinhuai River. The picture was taken in 1946.

places of decadence, but a singing woman could not attend school. Several reporters wrote articles condemning the incident.

In the 1910s and 1920s, singing women in Nanjing were made to wear badges of peach blossoms so as to distinguish themselves from private prostitutes. Finding the act derogatory, the women refused to wear the badges. Newspapers in the city engaged in a hot debate over the issue.

Although the order from the authorities was certainly discriminatory, an order was an order. Unhappy as they were, the women had to wear the badges in the end, for otherwise their business licenses could be annulled. With the breakout of the War of Resistance Against Japanese Aggression in 1937, the New Life Movement Commission in Nanjing decided to get rid of the profession of "drinking women" whose job

Wang Yurong,
singing-woman-turned
Peking opera actress

A singer with the name of Xiaohe who sang accompanied by a drum, an art form enjoyed by many Nanjingers in the early 20th century. In her early career she used to perform in competition with another famous singer, Bai Yunpeng, at the Confucius Temple. When Bai sang, the audience booed, but when Xiaohe sang, the audience burst into thunderous cheers for she was beautiful and her smile impressed every one. Her beauty, however, brought her trouble too. When men of lust could not get hold of her, they decided to destroy her. In the end, she married a merchant and disappeared from the stage.

Singing women on the Qinhuai seeking assistance from the women's society

it was to urge guests to drink more wine at dinners. Like singing women, they had also worn badges at work. Four months later, Nanjing fell to Japanese aggressors, something the New Life Commission could not have foreseen.

People enjoyed chitchatting about life and events on the Qinhuai River over a pot of tea, even in the simplest environment of an open air teahouse.

The Roads of Nanjing

The old stone road south of the Drum Tower, in 1888.

The earliest pictures taken of Nanjing that I have come across were shot in 1888. Without consulting the captions, I could tell what they were about. The one of the Drum Tower, for example, was probably taken from today's Zhujiang Road entrance, with the help of an old tripod and after much preparation. It has left us with a valuable shot of history. The photographer was apparently a foreigner. Sometimes a picture better explains things than does a long article. Today everybody is familiar with the fact that the section of Zhongshan Avenue from the Drum Tower to Xinjiekou

Residential houses
on both sides of the
Drum Tower

Though a new road had been completed, it still had to
go through the archway of the old city gate, 1990.

In 1930, the Drum
Tower had become the
center of a square.

is the most prosperous place in Nanjing, but no one
could have imagined that the area around the Drum
Tower would be this desolate some one hundred years
ago.

The date for the
taking of this picture of
the Drum Tower is not
clear.

What I find most interesting is the road paved with stone
slabs going through the archway of the Drum Tower. Once a
major thoroughfare, it zigzagged
its way from the riverside, link-
ing up the north and south of
the city. Such a stone surface
road is ideal for traveling on foot.
In the ancient past, all the roads
in Nanjing were like this one. According to *Random
Notes of Baixia*, "Stretching for miles from Shicheng
Gate to Tongji Gate, the road was paved with thick and
neatly cut stones.... It is a pity that they have been
damaged to what it looks like today by traveling carriages and oxen."

A wharf west of Zhonghua Gate, which was the west gate of the city of Nanjing. Beyond the arch gate was the prosperous district of the southern part of the city. It is not hard to imagine that at the time when the waterway was the major transportation line, the place must have been busy with activities.

Huimin Bridge, built in late Qing period, provided a major link between the road beginning at the riverside and leading into the city. This picture was taken in 1890.

The slab stone road built in the 14th century had been reduced to a poor condition by the end of the 20th century. Roads like this in a sense are the epitome of urban construction in ancient China. In 1894, the year of the Sino-Japan War, Zhang Zhidong, a leader of the Westernization faction in the Qing Dynasty government, decided to build a road that was modern by the standards of that time.

The new road began at the riverside, passing the Xiaguan docks and entering the inner city at Xingzhong Gate. It widened along the old slab stone road to the Drum Tower, turned east, going past the foot of the hill where the North Pole Pavilion stood, passing by the office of the government and presidential palace, and turning southwest to reach Tongji

The Yangtze River bank at Xiaguan, in 1888.

Gate. This was the first road in the real sense in the history of Nanjing. However, unlike the modern asphalt road of today, it was not very wide, no more than ten meters at the widest point and accessible only to rickshaws and horse-drawn carts.

Road building flourished along with the Westernization drive of the 19th century. Roads have always been one of the symbols of a civilization at any given time. The prosperous area in Nanjing at that time was along the Qinhuai River, while the Drum Tower was in the northern suburbs. By the last years of the Qing Dynasty, the Xiaguan docks further north had already become an important trading port. The Huimin River, running near the Yangtze, was connected with the Qinhuai River and tons of cargo was shipped to the southern part of the city from this position.

With the change of time, water transportation as part of the urban transportation system was gradually replaced by land transportation. Thus roads on land leading into the city suddenly gained in importance.

Xiaguan speedily changed its physical look after Nanjing became a trading port in 1899.

Regrettably, the small trains that were characteristic of land transportation in Nanjing could no longer be seen. The railroad for the small trains was built in 1907, taking a year and two months and costing only 400,000 taels of silver. Since the rails were slightly narrower than normal rails, residents of Nanjing fondly referred to the facilities as small trains. They operated for fifty years. At the beginning there were seven stops, namely Baixia Road where the palace of the president was located, Wuliang Nunnery near the Drum Tower, the North Pole Pavilion, the Dingjia Bridge, the Triple Archway Towers, and finally Xiaguan which should have been the end of the railroad. The road,

NO. One locomotive running on the small railway in Nanjing in the 1930s.

however, made a sudden turn to give rise to another stop called Jiangkou. It may sound strange, but the purpose for building this road was to transfer water to the office of the governor. As His Majesty the Governor wanted to drink the water from the Yangtze River, a "water tap house" was erected on the river bank and

the place name, Longtoufang (water tap house), is still in use today.

The Dingjia Bridge railway station

The small trains should not be overlooked as an urban means of transportation.

The urban railway went past the office of the viceroy of Anhui, Jiangxi, and Jiangsu provinces.

They greatly benefited the common people of Nanjing, particularly those who could not afford to ride in horse-drawn carriages or rickshaws. Besides, though the small trains began from the same location on

Zhongshan Avenue, which is the most important thoroughfare in Nanjing today, they did not cover the same route. A careful study of a map of Nanjing will show that prosperity in the city developed along Zhongshan

The small train went into the urban district through Jinchuan Gate.

Avenue. The areas the avenue progressed through gradually became the golden sections of the city. And it would have been quite possible to have two roads along such golden sections had the railroad not been dismantled.

There are many famous cities in the world that have not only maintained their railroads in urban districts but have even built tramways or trolley lines. When problems such as urban traffic congestion and environmental pollution began to trouble the city of Nanjing, the urban railroad there no longer existed. Perhaps to decision-makers, railways should only run in

A railway passing the Beijige in the City.

the vast expanse of land in the countryside. Residents living along the railways might have been unhappy at the loud noises created by the dashing trains. For a while, small railways and trains indeed became monsters in urban areas. Pedestrians often had to stop at the crossroads, waiting several minutes for the train to pass. And the simplest solution to the problem was to dismantle the rails and nobody at the time seemed to be aware of their values. Urban railways, ever after their construction, never had the chance to demonstrate their huge transport potentials. According to historical records, the greatest role that the Nanjing's small railways ever played was to transport the army and

The office of the viceroy of Anhui, Jiangxi, and Jiangsu later became the Palace of the Heavenly King during the Heavenly Kingdom period and the office and residence of the Nationalist government and president during the Republic period.

ammunition during the famous battle to defend Nanjing.

For Nanjing, which in fact is not very developed, the very existence of Zhongshan Avenue has allowed the city to be relatively free from the great pressures of urban transportation. Since the trains were sparse in between and the stations were distant from each other, more often than not they remained idle. The tragic dismantling of the small trains and the railroad was not because they had become too old and poor in condition, but rather because they were established too early when there was no scientific management available to run them.

Zhang Zhidong, viceroy of Anhui, Jiangxi, and Jiangsu, posing for a photo with Americans in 1895

Roads are the veins of a city. The best way to understand the history of a city is to make a study of the changes in its roads. When roads are developed, the look of the city invariably changes with them. The planners of urban Nanjing were quite far-sighted. Apart from the railroad, they also had Zhongshan Avenue, which remains a pride of the city to this day. This avenue consists of the North Zhongshan, Zhongshan, South Zhongshan and East Zhongshan Avenues. That tree-shaded thoroughfare that often brings fond memories to people's minds once provided enormous glory to the ancient city of Nanjing. At the very mention of Nanjing, people immediately think of its first-class greening effort that is best represented by the French parasol trees lining Zhongshan Avenue and on the central partitions of the streets. No one can tell how many French parasols there are in Nanjing, since many sections are embellished with as many as six rows of the trees, neatly stretching forward for miles and shading the roads from scorching sunshine. This luxury is not matched by any other city in China.

The riverside at Xiaguan in the 1930s. It was the starting point for several transportation thoroughfares.

People familiar with history are aware of the fact that road development in Nanjing had something to do with the "grand ceremony for laying the coffin" of Sun Yat-sen, respectfully known to the Chinese as father of the nation. In fact, the ceremony was only a pretext that gave Zhongshan Avenue the opportunity to come into being. Extending twelve kilometers, it was longer than Fifth Avenue in New York at the time and was then known as the "first avenue of the world." Having said that, it must be recognized that the construction of Zhongshan Avenue was no easy job. In 1925 Sun Yat-sen, whose Revolution of 1911 overthrew the Qing Dynasty, died in Beijing, then the national capital. At the time, the Beiyang (Northern) warlords were in power and the Kuomintang (Nationalists) under Sun Yat-sen, who served as the first provisional president of the young republic after the overthrow of the Qing Dynasty, was the party in opposition. What could be done for

The newly completed Zhongshan Avenue in 1929, with Xinjiekou at the crossroads

the former president was to have a mausoleum built on the Purple Hill in Nanjing, according to his own wishes expressed before his death. Funds for the construction of his mausoleum were donated from many quarters and it took four years to complete the construction in 1929. By that time the Kuomintang had already come to power, which enabled the completion of the first and second phases of the construction. The government that was now located in Nanjing held a solemn ceremony of laying down the coffin in the newly completed mausoleum. The final massive finishing touches of the project did not end until January 1932. Zhongshan Avenue, the construction of which took nine months to complete, actually was not part of the original plan for the mausoleum project.

The reason for this is that the Kuomintang urban construction authorities in Nanjing took the rare opportunity that the event presented to build up Nanjing, which served as the capital of the country under the reign of the Kuomintang. It seems that roads in Nanjing were destined to be related to the Xiaguan docks. This time, the road once again began from the riverside and took a slanting route to cut into the city from the northwest corner to the east of the city at the foot of Purple Hill.

Zhongshan Avenue dramatically changed the look of Nanjing. Its construction was a measure that held

A road for the passage of the remains of Sun Yat-sen was built in order to ship his coffin from Beijing to the mausoleum in Nanjing.

Gate and trees newly installed on the road along which the coffin of Sun Yat-sen was to go through. The young trees were specially ordered from the French concession in Shanghai.

On May 28, the coffin bearing the remains of Sun Yat-sen was shipped from Beijing to Pukou, Nanjing by a special train. At noontime, the coffin was ferried across the Yangtze River by the warship *Weisheng*. The picture shows the arrival of the coffin in Xiaguan.

the fate of the city and brought endless advantages. It, however, also inflicted many hardships on the residents in the city. As the task of construction was arduous and the time short, some details were left unconsidered. Many stores and residential houses along the route of construction were forcibly demolished, leaving many without shelter. The residents organized a protest group to parade and conduct a sit-down demonstration, criticizing the city authorities for giving no thought to people's livelihood for the sake of building a road. They cited Sun Yatsen's teachings about caring for the people. Liu Jiwen, mayor of the Special City of Nanjing, was a man who ruled with an iron hand. He personally took men to the construction site to dismantle houses. He also cited words from Sun Yat-sen, saying that road building was a prerequisite to developing the city and that what he was doing was to "carry out the teachings" of the former president. He said that purpose was to "build Nanjing into a city with artistic taste."

The Nobel laureate Pearl Buck, the US author who wrote *The Good Earth* in Nanjing, expressed great indignation at the behavior of the Nanjing authorities at the time. Several years later, however, she had to admit that the physical transformation of Nanjing was successful and that it was an obvious fact that road building did benefit the local residents.

Another foreign writer, Israel Epstein, also wrote about his impressions of Nanjing, which he compared to a government seat with Prussian taste, and yet he described Nanjing as a new magnificent capital. In his eye, Nanjing was like a Western city that was by no means less glamorous than many other capitals in the world. In order to build this road, residents did suffer hardships and the urban authorities made many

West end of East Zhongshan Avenue in 1935

enemies. However, the benefit that the project brought to the city and its people can still be felt by residents even today.

First there had to be the avenue, then the trees planted along its sides. When the trees grew up, people of later times could enjoy the cool shade. You have to admit that the officials who had Zhongshan Avenue built did a great project with great vision and the road stands as testimony to their virtue. The insight of the city authorities of those days should really be an example for later officials to follow. When people have the right idea, the change of the look of a city will not be far from happening.

Zhongshan Avenue completely changed Nanjing. For many years after that, the city stayed in the front ranks among cities in China in terms of road conditions. Though many French parasol trees had to be cut for city construction in the 1990s, Nanjing had few rivals among Chinese cities in terms of roadside tree and flower planting.

Now, returning to the small railroad mentioned earlier, if the road still existed today, it would have formed another major city trunk transportation line together with Zhongshan Avenue. Perhaps after modern transformation coupled with scientific management, and complimented with overpasses, transportation in

Liu Jiwen, mayor of Nanjing, was a rather charming official. When building Zhongshan Avenue, the military headquarters office happened to be on the way. To establish his authority, Liu decided to take the army office as an example and compelled the army to relocate its headquarters, resulting in compliance of many other government agencies.

East Zhongshan Avenue in 1936

East Zhongshan
Avenue in the 1940s

Nanjing might have had an entirely different situation, allowing smooth traffic while maintaining much of the original look of the ancient city, with many of the old French parasol trees preserved.

Were that the case, the city of Nanjing would have been unique. Such terms as international and cosmopolitan, to be sure, would have been reserved for places like Beijing and Shanghai, while Nanjing would have been an elegant and beautiful city where people would have put comfort in the environment above anything else. It would have been like what the stubborn mayor Liu Jiwen said: the city would not have been a forest of concrete, but "a city with artistic taste."

Hanzhong Road was completed in 1932 but the photo showing its disorderliness was taken in 1935.

Zhonghua Road, a major thoroughfare in the southern part of the city, used to be a prosperous place. The photo was taken in the early 1930s.

Taiping Road was rebuilt in 1931 and the photo was taken in 1937. During the occupation of Japanese aggressors, both Taiping and Zhonghua roads were badly damaged.

Xinjiekou Square in the early 20th century

The plan for Nanjing, capital of the Nationalist government, was meticulous and magnificent. This photo shows one corner in the eastern part. On the left of Huangpu Road was the Central Hospital while on the right was a cultural society. This photo was taken in 1935.

This road in Nanjing in the late 1940s had quickly recovered from damages incurred during the wars.

A picture of public buses taken in 1933. On January 1, 1929, Nanjing Zhenyu Bus Company hired over twenty women conductors. The measure met with ridicule from hypocrites who argued that men and women should not work on the same bus. The capital public security bureau declared that they had to be dismissed on the grounds that women conductors "were poor in health, lacked education, could not protect passengers, and might be objects of bullying by rogue youth." This order was later rescinded as a result of public pressure. From then on, women conductors began to serve on the city's buses.

Ma Chaojun served as mayor of Nanjing for three terms in the early 20th century, making his share of contributions to the construction of Nanjing.

In spring, Mayor Ma Chaojun took part in tree planting.

Ceremonies at the Sun Yat-sen Mausoleum

On December 1911, representatives from seventeen provinces that had announced independence from the Qing regime cast their votes in Nanjing. This picture shows the representatives. Each province had one vote and out of three candidates, Sun Yat-sen was elected provisional president of the young republic with sixteen votes.

The Revolution of 1911 broke out on September 10. At that time Sun Yat-sen, known as father of the Republic of China, was in the United States raising funds for the revolution. It was high time for the Qing Dynasty to perish and the revolution was bound to occur. However, nothing could happen without money. Though he did not personally take part in or lead the Wuchang Uprising, Sun's ideas provided the decisive role, while the money he raised provided the material guarantee. According to *South Sea Overseas Chinese Revolutionary History*, in 1911 the money donated by overseas Chinese living in the region of South China Sea alone amounted to 5 to 6 million yuan.

At the time, communications were by no means as developed as they are today. Sun Yat-sen learned the exciting news of the breakout of the revolution while he was thumbing through US newspapers. Immediately he decided to return to China via Britain and France. On December 25, he arrived in Shanghai. During the

Sun Yat-sen had this photo taken in Shanghai before he went to Nanjing to assume the provisional presidency.

two months that had just passed, revolutionaries fought bravely, shedding blood, against the Qing regime. Provinces declared independence one after another, leaving the Qing court utterly isolated.

On December 29, representatives from seventeen provinces that had declared independence from the Qing rule elected Sun Yat-sen provisional president of the Republic of China. From the facial expressions of the representatives shown in the photograph, they were apparently aware that because of their action China now had its first ever elected president.

Three days later, on New Year's Day of 1912, Sun left Shanghai to take up his post in Nanjing. Upon his departure, another photo was taken in which people are seen wearing rather serious expressions. China had entered the era of a republic, but if the Qing court could really be overthrown once and for all still depended on their further efforts.

I am not sure if this was the first time Sun came to Nanjing. Ever since then, however, the city had become inseparable from memory of him. On the third day of his arrival, he called the first cabinet meeting and appointed military and civil officials. On January 22, he solemnly declared that if the Qing emperor agreed to abdicate, he would resign and turn over his presidency to Yuan Shikai, who held military power in the country. On February 12, the last emperor of the Qing Dynasty declared his abdication and ordered Yuan to organize his provisional republican government. Taking the opportunity, Yuan issued a telegraph in which he expressed his support to the republic. Sun then responded by resigning to the provisional senate.

Only a few more than forty days after Sun Yat-sen became the provisional president, as the greatest winner of the Revolution of 1911, the shrewd and crafty Yuan Shikai was elected the new provisional president by the senate on February 25. To hand over the fruit of the revolution to Yuan was undoubtedly a mistake on the part of the revolutionaries. And to pay for their mistake, they incurred sacrifices greater than those of overthrowing the Qing Dynasty. "The revolution is yet to win success and comrades still have to strive

On January 3, 1912, Sun presided over the first cabinet meeting in Nanjing.

The shrewd and calculating Yuan Shikai, who had been
dismissed by the Qing court, captured the opportunity of the
Revolution of 1911 to make a comeback to the political stage. The
picture was taken before his comeback.

When Yuan became the provisional president, the fruit of the revolution was easily transferred into his hand. With great regret over what had happened, the revolutionaries later on referred to him as the thief of state power.

forward" was the call Sun issued to revolutionaries after realizing what had happened.

After assuming the presidency, Sun took all the officials, civil or military, to the mausoleum of Zhu Yuanzhang with the title of Taizu, founding emperor of the Ming Dynasty, located in Nanjing. He made a speech there in which he called for national unification. He had a picture taken in front of the mausoleum from which we can recognize the respect Sun had for the man who founded the Ming Dynasty in Nanjing centuries before. Soon after this event, when Sun and his colleagues went on a hunting trip to the Zhongshan Hill (also known as the Purple Hill) he said to them, "When I die, I would like to be buried here." It was the first time that he revealed his wish of enjoying the eternal rest on the Purple Hill. Thirteen years later when he was fatally ill, he once again expressed on his deathbed the desire of being buried on the Purple Hill. Given

74-64-1 On February 5, 1912, Sun Yat-sen took his officials, civil and military, to pay their respects at the Xiaoling Mausoleum, tomb of the founding emperor of the Ming Dynasty.

This picture was taken after the ceremony of paying respect to the first emperor of the Ming Dynasty.

Sun Yat-sen posing for a photo after giving a speech in front of the portrait of Zhu Yuanzhang, founding emperor of the Ming Dynasty.

On March 10, 1912, Sun Yat-sen went on a hunting trip to the Purple Hill where he expressed the wish to be buried on the hill when he eventually died.

the fact that Sun was the founding father of the republic, a state funeral was only too natural. The Beiyang (Northern) warlord government, despite its disagreements on many issues with the Kuomintang, had no way to refuse burying Sun in Nanjing.

For a time after his death in Beijing, Sun's coffin was laid for temporary rest in Biyun Temple in the

The photo was taken before Sun went to hand in his resignation of the provisional presidency to the senate.

Sun Yat-sen leaving the presidential palace after turning in his resignation

Western Hills of Beijing. The Kuomintang leadership, headquartered in Guangzhou, began to raise money, select a site, formulate the design, issue bids, and lay the corner stone for the construction of the tomb for Sun. Running into obstacles at every turn, the project progressed very slowly. Planned for completion within a year, it finally took more than three years to finish. Before the Kuomintang took the power and made Nanjing the national capital, the city was under the rule of the Beiyang (Northern) warlords and it is not

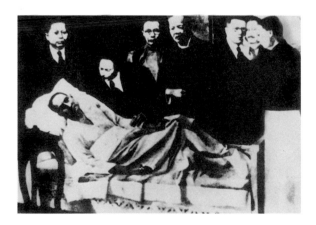

On March 12, 1925, Sun died at his residence in Tieshizi Lane, Beijing.

At his memorial ceremony were Sun Yat-sen's wife Soong Ching Ling, his son Sun Ke and his grandson Sun Zhiping.

difficult to imagine the problems there were in building Sun's tomb under the close watch of the warlord regime.

A reporton selecting the site for the mausoleum dated April 11, 1925.

Fortunately, in the years after Sun's death, his party, the Kuomintang (Nationalists), quickly grew in strength. Soon the National Revolutionary Army chiefly under the Kuomintang launched its northern expedition, conquering Wuchang in Central China, taking Nanchang in Eastern China, and fighting their way into Shanghai and Nanjing. In April 1927, the Nationalist government was formally established in Nanjing.

The series of victories of the National Revolutionary Army led to the Beiyang (Northern) warlord regime to conclude that it must be because of the blessings of the remains of Sun Yat-sen, now still in Beijing, that had given their opponent the key to victory. Some of the warlords thus suggested to have Sun's remains destroyed so as to rid the Nationalists of their blessing. Harassment from the warlord region led the people guarding Sun's remains, who feared physical destruction of the remains, to remove the body from the crystal coffin into a smaller coffin so that it could be hidden in a small mountain cave. This led to the intrusion of air into the crystal coffin and the abandonment of the plan to keep the deceased leader in the coffin eternally for the public to view so as to express their esteem and love.

The success of the Northern Expedition and the pronouncement of Nanjing as the capital of the Nationalist government provided the conditions for Sun's mausoleum to be completed. When Zhang Xueliang, one of the warlords, decided to place his army under the command of the Nationalist government, the other warlords finally realized that the unification of the country was inevitable and Nanjing became the capital of the entire nation in the true sense. This was precisely one of the cherished hopes of Sun Yat-sen. Bringing Sun's remains from Beijing to Nanjing for proper burial was one of the most important and solemn ceremonies in the history

The picture was taken when Soong Ching Ling and Sun Ke, wife and son of Sun Yat-sen, went to the Purple Hill together with representatives of the memorial committee to pick the site of his burial.

Sun Yat-sen Mausoleum under construction

The northbound train carrying the remains of Sun Yat-sen conducted a cross-country publicity campaign. The train was posted with quotations and a history of Sun Yat-sen.

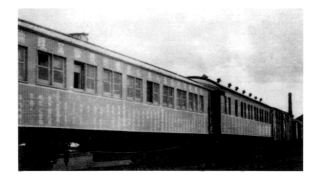

of the republic. In its wake, one ceremony followed another as the mausoleum of Sun Yat-sen became the stage for veneration by people of all nationalities and ethnic groups.

The camera lens captured the scene of the solemnity of the time. It was a good opportunity for the government in Nanjing to publicize itself. And the pomposity and extravagance went counter to the plain style of living that Sun Yat-sen advocated all his lifetime. The coffin laying ceremony was held on June 1, 1929, but for a month before that a great publicity campaign for the event was conducted. The most creative measure was the assembling of a train to publicize the event. The train with twelve blue carriages displayed instructions from Sun Yat-sen and a portrayal of history. It traveled from south to north across four provinces, stopping at thirty-three stations to publicize the event to a million

The northbound train carrying the remains of Sun Yat-sen

Chiang Kai-shek and his wife Soong May-ling among the entourage following the coffin bearing the remains of Sun Yat-sen

people along the way. Wherever the train stopped, local government officials and people's representatives came out to greet it and send it off. At each place, a rally was held and speeches were made eulogizing Sun's character and thought. A movie *The Life of the President* was shown at each stop.

A Guidance to Secondary School Education, published at the time, said in explicit language: "Nanjing was the capital picked by the former president." The plan of the Nanjing government was very clear, that is, to make use of the strong influence of Sun Yat-sen and the existence of his mausoleum in Nanjing to inculcate the idea that the country was under the rule of none other then the Kuomintang, and Nanjing was the only capital of the country.

Ever since its completion, the Sun Yat-sen Mausoleum has been an important symbol. The elaborate ceremony for laying the coffin signaled the end of the divided rule by warlords and the rise of a unified nation. The name list of the committee for the ceremony put together such names as Chiang Kai-shek, Hu Hanmin, Feng Yuxiang, Zhang Xueliang, Kong Xiangxi, Yu Youren and Lin Sen. But neither the name list nor the pomposity of the ceremony could hide the fact that the Kuomintang was a divided party. Wang Jingwei who was then in Paris, France; the Guangxi faction; Feng Yuxiang and Yan Xishan, who both had under their command a strong military; all bore strong grudges against the government in Nanjing under the rule of Chiang Kai-shek. Had Zhang Xueliang not thrown his support to Chiang during the clashes between the factions eight months after the coffin laying ceremony, it might have been another question as to who would have been the final victor instead of Chiang.

At 8:00 am on June 1, 1929, people gathered at the appointed place in front of the mausoleum for the coffin laying ceremony.

Among the photos of people paying their respects at the mausoleum, we can see Chiang pictured together with Zhang Xueliang, taken right after the end of the fighting among Chiang, Feng, Yan, and the Guangxi factions. Because of his contribution in rendering Chiang support in the conflict, Zhang was made deputy commander-in-chief of the ground, air, and navy forces. He also became a sworn brother of Chiang Kai-shek. Territories formerly under Feng and Yan, including such provinces as Hebei, Beijing and Tianjin, were all put under Zhang's command. In the picture, we find Chiang wearing a stern expression but one with a revelation of happiness over his victory, for the war that had just ended had proved that nobody in the country was his rival in military strength. After that, Zhang became Chiang's only trusted officer in guarding China's territory. In 1931, when Japan invaded China's northeast, Chiang adopted a non-resistance policy so as to concentrate on the civil war against the Red Army. As a result of this policy, Zhang lost the entire three provinces in the northeast almost before he realized it. Six years later, it was Zhang who was sent to the northwest to wipe out the Red Army. He then turned against Chiang's non-resistance policy by launching the Xian Incident in which he compelled Chiang to give up his policy and unite with the Red Army to fight the Japanese aggressors.

On November 12, 1930, Chiang Kai-shek and Zhang Xueliang took civil and military officials to pay respects to Sun Yat-sen at his mausoleum.

The fond plan of Chiang in suppressing domestic opponents first before warding off foreign invasion was now smashed by none other than his sworn brother, Zhang Xueliang. No wonder people used to remark that it was the same Zhang who had helped Chiang to realize his dream first and then also smashed his dream later on. The peaceful ending of the Xian Incident actually advanced Chiang's reputation and popularity, as he promised to fight Japan from then on. When he returned to Nanjing from Xian, he was greeted with firecrackers. The fact that Chiang, who died in Taiwan in 1975, neither killed nor released Zhang (who died in Hawaii in 2001 after almost a life-long house-arrest) was the result of Zhang's support to Chiang during the latter's war against Feng, Yan, and the Guangxi warlords and his later capture of Chiang in Xian to compel him to change the non-resistance policy. Their relationship, filled with love and hate, was a decisive factor in the historical process of China.

To attend memorial services at Sun Yat-sen Mau-

The Chiangs and Zhangs

soleum has been a special activity in Nanjing. In fact, even before the mausoleum was completed, it was already a fad for people to go and pay their respects. Many visitors to the city took the bus to show their respect at the mausoleum when it was still under construction. At the time, the construction site was a pile of scaffolds, roaring with machinery, in the barren surroundings of the hill. People went to such a place because they loved and respected Sun Yat-sen. They went also because of what they had read in the newspapers, hoping to see with their own eyes a magic project in the architectural history of the country. Even before the coffin laying ceremony, the Nationalist government was already busy organizing respect paying activities. For example, representatives to the National Conference on Education held in May 1928 and the National Conference on Finance held in July the same year were brought to the site for a memorial service. After the coffin laying ceremony, memorial services at

During the 1930s, trees at Sun Yat-sen Mausoleum had not yet grown tall, making the site's wide and long stairway an ideal location for public gatherings and ceremonies.

the mausoleum quickly became one of the most important events in Nanjing. Almost all important conferences included on their agenda such a memorial service. Some conferences even had their opening ceremony at the mausoleum.

Apart from memorial days, the coffin chamber of the mausoleum was open only on Sundays. In the years following the coffin laying ceremony, tens of thousands of people visited the mausoleum each year at a time when there was no such thing as tourism. So the number of visitors at the time was really something compared to the one million a year that go there today when tourism is a prosperous industry. So the Sun Yat-sen Mausoleum, as a popular site for various ceremonies, has long been a place for providing people with spiritual consolation and urgings.

After a heavy snowfall in the winter of 1935, Fan Xuting, a Kuomintang lieutenant general, tried to commit suicide by stabbing himself in the stomach at the

Making use of the memorial activities marking the anniversary of Sun Yat-sen's death on March 12, 1936, students from Nanjing Middle School cried fervently in front the mausoleum, demanding that the government adopt a policy of resistance against the Japanese invaders. On June 10, students held a demonstration, marching in front of the Japanese embassy. The school was later dismissed on the grounds of "extreme" actions of the students.

mausoleum. Though he was rescued, the event exerted a strong impact, because his purpose in doing so was to protest against the Nanjing government's policy of not sending troops to resist Japanese invaders now rolling into North China. After this incident, resisting Japan became the major part of public opinion in the country, throwing Chiang in a rather awkward situation. The suicide incident was a prelude to the Xian Incident a year later, making it clear that a war between China and Japan was unavoidable. Two years later the curtain of the anti-Japanese war of aggression was lifted with great heroism. As the Japanese aggressors approached Nanjing, Chiang Kai-shek made a quick goodbye in front of the mausoleum. What followed was the tragic Nanjing Massacre.

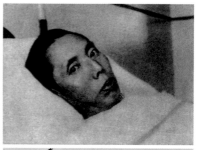

Lieutenant General Fan Xuting after being rescued

War, however, did not inflict fatal destruction on the Sun Yat-sen Mausoleum. Even during Japanese occupation, memorial services at the mausoleum did not reduce in number but became even more frequent and had a greater number of attendants. After his death in Beijing, Sun Yat-sen was given an autopsy and his liver was made into a specimen to be kept at the Union Hospital in Beijing. When the war in the Pacific broke out, the Japanese occupants transferred the specimens in the hospital to the renegade regime under Wang Jingwei, who made a great show with an elaborate ceremony of "placing the remains of the father of the nation to rest." They put the liver in a glass container and placed it in

Note Fan Xuting wrote before his suicide attempt

Japanese aggressors occupied Sun Yat-sen Mausoleum.

Zhang Jinghui, one of the chief renegade officials, went to pay his respects at the Sun Yat-sen Mausoleum. He was dressed like a Japanese officer.

German and Italian military officers visited the mausoleum.

Foreign envoys visited the mausoleum.

the mausoleum at Nanjing for public viewing. After this renegade regime was overthrown at the end of the war against Japan, Chu Minyi, one of the chief renegades, removed the liver to use as leverage in asking his pardon from the Nationalist government. His action aroused strong public indignation and condemnation against a renegade who had committed serious crimes of treason against his own nation and now wanted to trade the liver for his freedom.

Chu Minyi, a major official of the renegade regime under Japanese rule, was sentenced to death.

Eight years of fighting against the Japanese aggressors after Chiang shed tears in goodbye at the mausoleum in December 1937, the Nationalist government now returned to Nanjing. Naturally, there was a grand ceremony marking the event. And the venue for the ceremony was the mausoleum. The event proved to be the most solemn one at the site ever since the coffin laying ceremony in 1929. Smartly dressed in military attire with a pair of snow white gloves, Chiang Kai-shek, in a happy mood and with a walking stick in hand, ascended the rostrum in light steps, with his wife Soong May-ling close by and in the company of many others. According to reports, the ceremony was grand in style with hundreds of limousines parked at the entrance to the mausoleum and thirty-six Kuomintang flags and national

On May 5, 1946, a grand ceremony was held at the Sun Yat-sen Mausoleum marking the return of the Nationalist government to Nanjing from the wartime capital of Chongqing.

flags fluttering on both sides of the path leading to the mausoleum. Civil officials either in Sun Yat-sen style suits or traditional Chinese robes took the stairs on the left while military officials taking the right stairs all wore full military uniforms. The center of the stair path was

On May 5, 1947, more than four hundred high-ranking officers cried in front of the Sun Yat-sen Mausoleum as a way to express their disagreement with Chiang who reduced the strength of other factions of the armed forces under the pretext of a military reorganization.

Before the Communist Party delegation to the peace negotiations departed from Nanjing in the wake of the breakdown of the talks, Zhou Enlai, leader of the delegation, had this picture taken in front of the Sun Yat-sen Mausoleum.

Deputies to the National Assembly paid their respects to Sun Yat-sen at his mausoleum.

reserved for Chiang alone. It was the most glorious moment in his career, but also a turning point marking the change from his prime leadership to his decline. History recorded the moment when he came down from the mausoleum.

Six months from the end of 1946, the negotiations for peace between the Communists and the Nationalists broke down. Before the Communist delegation left Nanjing, they made a special trip to pay their respects to Sun Yat-sen at his mausoleum. Zhou Enlai, leader of the delegation, had a picture taken in front of the mausoleum. What people did not recognize at the time was that this unusual ceremony heralded the lifting of the curtain on a decisive war of unprecedented scale and significance. The Communist forces, inferior to the Kuomintang forces in number and arms, eventually emerged as the victors while Chiang Kai-shek, who had shortly before returned to Nanjing in glory and pomposity, now became the actor of another tragedy—— fleeing Nanjing after bowing in front of the Sun Yat-sen Mausoleum with a gloomy face. His destination this time was Taiwan.

Chiang Kai-shek left Nanjing for good.

The Lost Dreams
of College

Graduation Record of Class 22 of Central University

I was overwhelmed by what I read while turning the pages of a faxed copy of a document titled *Graduation Record of Class 22 at Central University.* As a late comer to that same university, I found the book particularly endearing as I examined the pictures of my predecessor-alumni.

It seems that Nanjing was born to be a place for students and scholars who made Nanjing their home in times of peace as well as during years of difficulty. For ages the Confucian Temple had been the center of Nanjing, serving as the venue for imperial examinations and an outpost for scholars studying to aspire to a better future. The city, sitting on the banks of the

Yangtze River, linked up the surrounding regions. The Ming Dynasty alone saw more than 10,000 students studying at the Imperial College which was then the institute for the highest learning in the country. *The Yongle Dictionary*, which consists of more than 22,900 volumes, is believed to have been compiled here.

Interestingly, although the Ming Dynasty Imperial College was established right after the powerful Ming emperor took control of the country, institutions of higher learning in the modern sense did not emerge until the overthrow of the Qing Dynasty in the early 20th century. Since they were established at different times, these institutions varied in purpose and significance. The founding of institutions of higher learning in Nanjing in the early 20th century were based on the ideas of patriotism and rejuvenation of the nation. When discussing institutions of higher learning in Nanjing, some names need to be mentioned. The first person to remember is Zhang Zhidong, founder of Sanjiang Normal College, who then became viceroy of Anhui, Jiangsu, and Jiangxi

Jiangnan Gongyuan, an imperial examination center during the feudal dynastic times.

兩江師範學堂全圖

A sketch of the LiangJiang Normal College drawn in 1907

provinces. The booklet marking the Tenth Anniversary of the National Central University says in its very first line: "Sanjiang Normal College was established by Mr. Zhang Zhidong in 1902."

Zhang was a key person in pushing the ancient city of Nanjing into the modern age. Sanjiang Normal College was a starter, predecessor of the Central University and today's Nanjing University and Southeast University. Without Sanjiang Normal College and without such an enlightened person as Zhang Zhidong there would have been no institutions of higher learning to speak of in Nanjing. It seems everything was destined to be what it was. The location of the Sanjiang Normal College was at the very place of the Imperial College during the Ming Dynasty. The *East Magazine* published in 1904 describes the Sanjiang Normal College in this way: "College buildings are Western in style. The roads are wide. The cost for construction was no less than what was spent on building Tokyo

A photo of the co-founders of Sanjiang Normal College. Sitting in the center is Zhang Zhidong, governor of Liangjiang (Anhui, Jiangsu, and Jiangxi provinces).

University in Japan. The college is still under construction for completion scheduled in the fall next year."

Simply put, the emergence of institutions of higher learning was part of the Westernization drive in China. For years China had been in a backward position, and being backward meant being beaten. So people came to realize that there was the necessity of introducing a new kind of education. To learn from the West involved many difficulties and people began learning from the example of Japan, which had been successful in learning from the West. At the very start, Sanjiang Normal College invited eleven teachers from Japan. At that time there were only seventy students. For a long time China learned from the West indirectly through Japan. In fact, the first teachers introduced from Japan all taught courses about the West.

The second person that should be mentioned is Li Ruiqing, a noted contemporary educator and calligrapher. His theories were crystallized into the maxim of the college: "Endure hardships and aspire to

In 1903, Sanjiang Normal College changed its name to Liangjiang Normal College, and in 1915 once again it changed its name to Nanjing Higher Normal School. The photo shows students and teachers with US educator John Dewey in 1919.

make great achievements." Very soon Sanjiang (Three-river) Normal College changed its name into Liangjiang (Two-river) Normal College. Under Li's stewardship, Liangjiang quickly grew in size and his students acquired the fine tradition of learning well. Many of his students emerged as outstanding talents, including the authoritative scholar of Chinese studies Hu Xiaoshi and famous fine art educator Lu Fengzi. Li commanded great respect because he "treated education as his life, the school as his family, and students as his kinsmen." Besides, he stayed away from politics.

After the breakout of the Revolution of 1911 aimed at overthrowing the Qing Dynasty, Zhang Xun, governor of Jiangning appointed by the Qing court, killed every revolutionary he arrested. Li Ruiqing protected progressive students all he could.

When Nanjing was taken by the New Army, Cheng Dequan, commander of the New Army, wanted to keep Li Ruiqing as his adviser so that he might be able to enlist the service of talented people such as Li. Li, however, turned down the offer. After turning in thousands upon thousands of taels of silver under his care and a complete list of properties

Li Ruiqing, president of Liangjiang Normal College

and personnel of the college, he left the school. After that, he lived under a pseudonym, and tried to make a living by selling calligraphy and paintings. After learning his real identity, many people went to ask him to be their teacher so that they could learn the art of writing and painting from him. Zhang Daqian (Chang Ta-chien), a famous painter in the 20th century, was one of his proud students. After Li's death, he was buried at Ox Head Hill in Nanjing. On a scroll in memory of Li, Kang Youwei, a noted scholar and reformist at the time, wrote: "Having written outstanding works as a scholar widely known in south China, he lived in seclusion yet without becoming depressed. Having taught students all over the country, he lives in immortality with nothing more to be desired."

Li can be said to be a fine example of the best men of letters.

In the years following the Revolution of 1911, there was a popular belief that those interested in becoming officials went to Beijing, for that was the place where the Beiyang (Northern) warlord government was located. Those interested in making money flocked to Shanghai, for that was the place where foreigners lived. Those interested in learning went to Nanjing, for apart from books to read, there was nothing else. Reading became a part of the fine traditions of the ancient city of Nanjing, where people read under oil lamps well into the small hours. Nanjing indeed was the home of bookworms. Students in Nanjing of course were under the influence of the time, but their devotion to learning

Li Ruiqing's handwriting

"Plum Shrine," built in memory of Li Ruiqing

Entrance to Central University

Campus of Central
University

In order to become the number one university in the country, Central University emphasized a unique style in every way.

The Science Museum of Central University

Nanjing Higher
Normal School

N0. 4 Dormitory
Building of Central
University

A bus from the
Agriculture College of
Central University

far exceeded that of students elsewhere.

At the mention of the history of higher education, there is another name to be listed——Luo Jialun. People familiar with the history of the May 4th Movement of 1919 are aware that the most famous student leaders in organizing the May 4th demonstration in Beijing were Luo Jialun and Fu Sinian, who were idols of a generation of progressive students early in the 20th century. Mao Zedong who once served as a clerk at the Peking University library, expressed his respect for these two student leaders. Although both were pro-Kuomintang and had anti-Communist attitudes, and both went to Taiwan when the Communist Party took over the country, their role in history cannot be negated.

We mention Luo because he was a man of learning who had studied in universities of Princeton, Columbia, London, Berlin, and Paris. In 1932 he became president of the Central University, which was one of the key institutions of higher learning in China at the

Mr. Luo Jialun, president of Central University

Mr. Wang Xuchu, dean of humanities, Central University

Mr. Hu Xiaoshi

Mr. Huang Kan

Mr. Wang Bijiang

Mr. Wu Mei

time. Funds it had, disciplines it offered, and the number of its staff and students equaled the total of the combined figures in the same fields at Tsinghua, Jiaotong, Wuhan, and Zhejiang universities, which all commanded similar fame as that of Central University. It must be admitted, however, although Central University had more disciplines and the largest scale, it had its own difficulties and in more ways than one failed to live up to its reputation as the "university of the capital."

It was Luo's vigorous efforts that changed the difficult situation at Central University. In his inauguration speech, he pointed out that many of the problems in China were rooted "in the lack of a national culture strong enough to mobilize the national spirit," and thus it was the unswerving responsibility of institutions of higher learning to shoulder the "mission of creating a national culture." The atmosphere at Central University showed a drastic change for the better after he assumed his post as he united everybody in striv-

Left: Ms. He Shuli of the Department of Chinese
Middle: Ms. Shen Zufen, a student of Central University, whose work *An Analytical Study of Song Ci Poems* makes good reading.
Right: Ms. Long Yuan of the Department of Chinese

中文系的何淑梨女士。

中大女生沈祖棻女士，她的著作《宋词赏析》太值得读一下。

中文系的龙沅女士。

ing for a common goal-to quickly turn the university into a talent bank. Luo Jialun poured great effort into improving the quality of the teaching staff, recruiting talented people and placing them at what they did best. Many outstanding scholars, such as economist Ma Yinchu, painter Xu Beihong, agronomists Jin Shanbao and Cai Xu, astronomer Zhang Yuzhe, and medical scientist Cai Qiao were faculty members at the university. In 1933, the Science College alone had over a dozen leading scholars with a background of having received their education abroad.

Once Luo Jialun said that, "Recruiting people is what I pay the most attention to." There are quite a few stories about how he selected talented teachers when he was still the president of Tsinghua University. According to one, Mr. Qian Zhongshu, the respected 20th century scholar of literature, failed in math when he took the entrance exam into Tsinghua. He was enrolled only with special permission from Luo, giving rise to the classic story of how an able leader spotted a tal-

Left: Ms. Ren Bijun of the Department of Biology
Middle: Ms. Zhou Mai of the Department of Law
Right: Ms. Shou Jingru of the Department of Law

生物系的任碧筠女士。

法学系的周迈女士。

法学系的寿静如女士。

Professor Xu Beihong with his students at Central University in 1928

ented person. Luo was often compared with Bole, a man who lived in the Spring and Autumn Period, reputed to be able to spot good horses that would be particularly skilled at scouting talents. Naturally Bole also offended many people in doing so. The spirit of Central University "honesty, plain style, aspiration, and lofty ideals" coincided with what Li Ruiqing had advocated at Liangjiang Normal College: "Endure hardships and aspire to make great achievements."

Luo's goals were to turn Central University into China's Harvard, or Britain's Cambridge and Oxford. Since the most important issue was resisting Japanese aggression at that time, Luo often said that, "The target of resistance for Central University is Tokyo Imperial University of Japan." He further noted that Central University should catch up with and do better than Tokyo University "in science and other general disciplines." Indeed, Central University developed at astonishing speed and by the beginning of the War of Resistance Against Japanese Aggression it had bought over 530 hectares of land at today's Shizigang for building a new campus. A grand campus building plan was starting to be put into practice. The plans for actual construction were drawn and the major buildings for

The Choral Society
of Central University

the engineering and agricultural colleges were already
under construction. Several months later, however, the
war broke out, shattering Luo's grand design. Today,
the former site for the new campus of the Central University is the Nanjing crematory. What a disheartening change!

Central University did not shirk the responsibility
of being first among the Chinese universities. In the
early 1940s, the ministry of education enlisted a number of senior professors as special scholars of the
ministry. Among the first two groups of forty-five such
professors, twelve or more than one-fourth were from
Central University, more in number than those from
any other university. During the war against Japan,
Chiang Kai-shek personally served as the school's
president and later as permanent honorary president.
Despite the intrusion of bureaucratic influence onto
the university campus, Central University managed to

effectively ward off the growth of wrongdoing thanks to its fine, strong traditions. To serve as the president of this university was like being the minister of education for the entire country. Zhu Jiahua, for example, was president of Central University for a year and then became minister of education. The great trend of "turning bureaucratic style into academic emphasis" left no place for those who wanted to use their academic studies as a jumping board into the bureaucratic world. At the end of the 1940s, thirty-three out of a total of eight-one academicians in the country either had studied or taught at Central University.

In the mind of true students, nothing is more important than one's academic position when it comes to judging the value of a particular person. From the alumni record, we see a large number of famous scholars who have been authorities or founding figures in various fields of studies. They include people occupying vital positions in institutions not only on China's mainland, but also in Hong Kong and Taiwan and even in Europe and North America. The head of Taiwan's ministry of education, the curator of Taiwan's Museum of Chinese History, and the president of Hong Kong University were once students at Central University. C. H.

The History Society of Central University

Wu, the first woman chairperson of the US Society of Physics, and the world-renowned geographer, Professor C. H. Hsu of the University of Technology in Switzerland, were also graduates of Central University. Graduates of the university all benefited directly from the healthy academic traditions of the university. It was precisely because of these traditions that Central University was able to bring up group after group of outstanding graduates. Though Luo's grand goals did not completely materialize, the academic traditions he helped establish and maintain are still worth advocating today.

A lab at Central University

Doing embry-
ological studies in a lab

A fine cattle stock
cultivated by the
Agriculture College of
Central University

To establish a good academic style is of vital importance. And good styles can lead to a noble spirit. During the difficult years when China suffered under foreign aggression, the spirit of devotion displayed by the bookworms who dedicated their time to academic studies was something the bureaucrats failed to provide. For instance, teachers of the Agriculture College of Central University overcame tremendous difficulties in taking fine-stock animals they had spent years cultivating out of Nanjing and traveling thousands of kilometers across Anhui Province to Shangcheng, in Henan Province to keep them out of the hands of the Japanese aggressors who were about to take over Nanjing. As these agricultural scholars traveled they were harassed by Japanese enemy planes overhead and pursuing troops behind. Sometimes they found themselves encircled by Japanese soldiers. Under such circumstances, however, these teachers did not give up or simply run for their lives. They made the journey without the means of transportation. To press ahead, they put the smallest animals such as chickens, ducks and rabbits into cages on the back of thee oxen, sheep and pigs that had been introduced from the United States, Holland, and Australia. They urged the animals to travel across hills and rivers, covering a mere several kilometers each day. When winter came, both men and animals were tired and cold. They had to tide over the winter in the wooded Tongbai Mountains and waited until the next spring to go on.

Students at the university did not give up their studies because of the war. They were fully aware that only by studying harder would there be a way to rescue the country and lift it out of its suffering. With the examples set by their teachers, the students took it as their major task to study. During the War of Resistance Against Japanese Aggression, the university moved west to Chongqing where the students maintained the tradition of hard work. They continued to lead stu-

Women students at Jinling Girls University washing their clothes in their spare-time, 1946

A costume ball by the students at Jinling Girls University, 1948

"Boy scouts of Central University," as original caption attached to the photo suggests.

dents in other universities in their academic achievements.

Once a good academic style has become an established tradition, it will not be easy to change. At the same time a bad habit will be hard to change. The joy brought by hard work is something those who do not work hard can never understand or appreciate. For a university, all wonderful projections will vanish like bubbles if its students do not work hard. During people's lifetime, there are not many opportunities for them to study hard to begin with. And if those valuable opportunities are not made the best use of, it is indeed a sad thing.

School badge of
Central University

Girl scouts

A student demonstration on Zhujiang Road. At 10:
50, May 20, 1947, the military police used water cannons
to stop the students from marching forward. Some of
the students tried to take away the water hoses from
the police.

The Flames of War Against Japanese Aggression

The model of a bomb erected at Xinjiekou Square, 1935

Residents in Nanjing today find it very hard to pinpoint the center of their city. The city is expanding. Prosperity is in evidence everywhere. And the traditional concept of the city center is changing. In the 1930s, however, the center for Nanjing residents was, without the slightest doubt, Xinjiekou. At that time, a huge model of a bomb was placed in Xinjiekou Square, a fact many people today still remember. I first came across this while reading the work of a foreigner by the name of Israel Epstein. At the time, I was immediately gripped by the question: Wasn't Chiang Kai-shek described as being non-resistant to Japanese aggression?

Chiang Kai-shek had always regarded imperial Japan as his opponent. People familiar with the history of the last century remember the tragedy of Jinan in 1928. They will remember that Chiang commanded the Northern Expedition that defeated the Beiyang (Northern) warlords, completing the great endeavor of uniting the north with the south of the country.

Anti-air raid exhibition inside First Park in Nanjing. Here there is also a model of a heavy bomb.

Regrettably, such glory was seriously tarnished. The most humiliating part was that in Shandong Province on its northbound march the Northern Expedition army was rudely intercepted by the Japanese army. The Japanese took the provincial capital of Jinan, killing more than four thousand civilians and army men and breaking into the Kuomintang's battlefield foreign affairs office where they arrested Cai Gongshi, special negotiator appointed by the Kuomintang government to

In May 1928, Japanese troops occupied Jinan. This picture shows Chinese prisoners held by Japanese soldiers. The incident was the first humiliation Japan slammed onto Chiang Kai-shek.

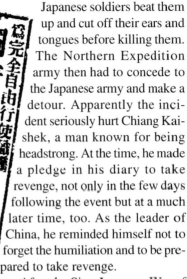

Shandong, along with sixteen others. The Japanese soldiers beat them up and cut off their ears and tongues before killing them. The Northern Expedition army then had to concede to the Japanese army and make a detour. Apparently the incident seriously hurt Chiang Kai-shek, a man known for being headstrong. At the time, he made a pledge in his diary to take revenge, not only in the few days following the event but at a much later time, too. As the leader of China, he reminded himself not to forget the humiliation and to be prepared to take revenge.

After the Sino-Japanese War of 1894, the Chinese people never stopped expressing their wish to resist Japan. Similarly, the Japanese imperialists never

On January 30, 1932, the Nationalist government moved its capital from Nanjing to Luoyang. As war did not immediately break out, it moved back to Nanjing in September. The picture shows the return of the government to Nanjing.

The picture above is a newspaper report on relocating the capital to Luoyang.

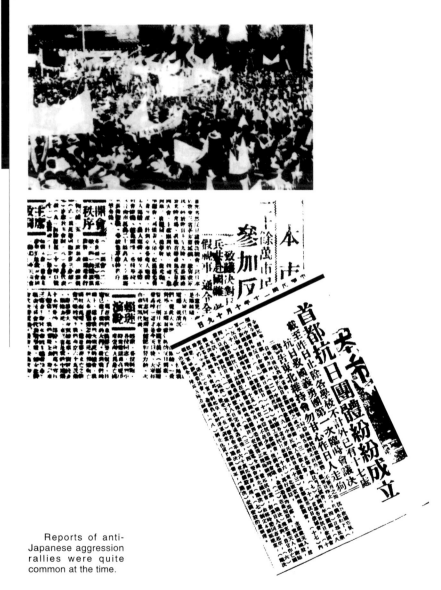

Reports of anti-Japanese aggression rallies were quite common at the time.

Resisting Japanese aggression was the theme of the time. The slogan reads "Sabotaging resistance against Japan is counterrevolutionary."

stopped trying to plunder China. As the two countries had become opponents, a war between them was bound to break out. Like Chiang, many professional army officers such as Sun Chuanfang, Yan Xishan and Cai E had studied military affairs in Japan and the purpose of their studies did not rule out the possibility of fighting a decisive war with Japan later on.

Three years after the Jinan Incident, the September 18 Incident that was even harder for the Chinese to

To boycott Japanese goods, as the slogan in this picture says, was one of the important patriotic actions.

swallow took place. The Japanese army had invaded and occupied the three northeastern provinces in 1931. Enraged, the Chinese people held demonstrations. Students in northern cities stopped trains, climbed onto them, and went down to Nanjing to ask for a battle of resistance. Chiang personally met with the students. His worried face seemed to indicate that he was moved by the students. In fact, for the nation, the old scar had hardly healed and now the new injury had been inflicted. He promised that the central armies would provide an answer to the patriotic students and so we see a photo with words of Chiang. He said in a sorrowful tone: "If soldiers are not dispatched to fight within three days, you can chop my head off as an answer to the nation."

On November 26, 1931, Chiang Kai-shek met with students and promised "If soldiers are not dispatched to fight within three days, you can chop my head off as an answer to the nation."

Making a speech at
a street corner

It was an absurd promise. It was not until six years later when the Chinese army under Chiang actually fought the Japanese invaders. By then in the spring of 1937, the Japanese aggressors had already thrust their swords into the throat of the Chinese nation. Only then did Chiang's army hurriedly respond to the invaders. To say the least, the promise Chiang made in 1931 was not serious enough.

According to historical records, on September 22, 1931, four days after the September 18th Incident in which China lost the three northeastern provinces to Japan, Chiang, freshly back from the frontline in encir-

Exterior of an anti-
air raid exhibition

cling the Red Army under the Communist Party, spoke in the auditorium of Central University and promised to recover the lost territory in three months. If the land was not recovered, he said he would personally go to the front to block the gun barrels of the Japanese invaders. At the time, one of the students in the audience, someone from a military academy, did not believe him. The student shouted: "Don't overstate yourself." This caught the entire audience by surprise. Someone immediately rushed over and pulled the poor student onto the stage. The indignant Chiang slapped him on the face twice in public and then made him bow three times in front of a portrait

Publicizing knowledge on anti-air raid at Zhonghua Road

A capital anti-air raid plan was drawn in 1931 and was improved several times later on. Here Yang Jie, commander of the capital anti-air raid forces, is reviewing the anti-air raid troop in 1935.

convoy of vehicles during an anti-air raid military exercise in 1934

Winners of an anti-air raid speech contest

of Sun Yat-sen. This incident demonstrated that Chiang lacked the style of a true leader and was more like a swordsman or a vagrant.

Chiang was more devoted to fighting the civil war. And China, in fact, lacked a real national defense force to fight imperial Japan. To resist Japan and salvage the nation was the popular theme in the 1930s, under which

Wife of an army general issuing an award to a winner of an anti-air raid speech contest. These pictures indicate that the Nationalist government at least had made some preparations for the war against Japan. Preparations, however, did not mean that the government was truly ready for war.

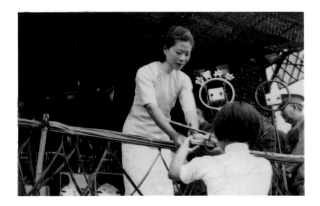

Nanjing after being
bombed by Japan

it was no wonder that a model of a huge bomb was
erected in Nanjing, capital of the country. To correspond with the bomb, the Nationalist government also
erected a so-called "Hindenburg defense line" to pre-
vent Japanese troops from rolling onto Nanjing from
the concessions in Shanghai. Residents were mobi-
lized and there were endless speeches on anti-air raid
defense. People rushed to buy air defense lotteries and
young teachers went to the suburbs to perform plays
with anti-Japanese themes. Everywhere you could hear

On November 20,
1937, the Nationalist
government announced
that it would make
Chongqing the capital.
In early December, the
battle to defend Nanjing
began. On December
13, Japanese troops
broke open the defense
at Zhonghua Gate and
Japanese tanks rolled
into the city.

Japanese troops killed residents in Nanjing like flies.

voices calling for resistance to Japan and the salvaging of the nation.

For people in Nanjing, the Marco Polo Bridge Incident on July 7, 1937 did not mean the beginning of the war, for the bridge was in the north, far away from Nanjing, where people were already used to provocation from the north. For people in Nanjing, the incident on August 13, 1937 lifted the curtain to the anti-Japanese war. The impressions people got from newspapers full of stories of victories was that the Chinese army, magically quick, was driving the Japanese invaders into the sea. During the initial days of the war, secondary school students in Nanjing waged a movement to donate 50,000 towels to the soldiers on the front, but the organizers actually received only forty-nine in total, indicating that even at this junction in history, most people could not believe that war was already being waged.

People appeared to be supportive of the government's efforts, but the real impact of the war had not yet reached them. Patriots referred to their attitude as "five-minute political enthusiasm." Everything seemed to be in place before the war actually broke out, but once the first shots were fired, people were at

The swastika flag mentioned in *The Good Man of Nanjing: The Diaries of John Rabe*

a loss as what to do. On August 15th, two days after the incident of August 13, 1931, Japanese planes appeared in the sky over Nanjing.

The Japanese troops then proudly and arrogantly marched into the city of Nanjing, resulting in mass destruction and killing, as entire streets were set on fire, civilians were murdered, and women raped. I am not going to go into the details of the Nanjing Massacre here, as people can read about it in any book and see pictures revealing the atrocity of that event. The disaster Nanjing suffered is a fact no one could deny.

One of the pictures in a recently published book, *The Good Man of Nanjing: The Diaries of John Rabe*, shows Rabe hoisting a German National Socialist Party flag six meters long and three meters wide in his compound in Nanjing. On the flag is a huge swastika, a symbol that would warn Japanese planes to stay away. The Nationalist army could not protect people and the ancient city with a history of a thousand years had to rely on a German Nazi flag to protect its people from being bombed by Japan. Some people refer to Rabe as China's Schindler. Later he became the chief person responsible for helping refugees. Thanks to his efforts, many Chinese were saved from death under the most difficult circumstances. Rabe was a witness to history and a Don Quixote type of a person in his time. It was his knightly spirit and gallantry that made it possible for many to escape disasters. As a German citizen and

With the fall of Nanjing, people rushed into refugee camps. This picture shows women in a refugee district.

a resident of Nanjing, he left behind a great deal of valuable first-hand material.

We may, as well, take a look at a poster of the Japanese army collected in Rabe's book. It is a picture that makes one's heart ache. It shows a fully armed Japanese soldier holding a Nanjing child in his arm.

日本軍隊極力保護良民
使其安居樂業不過對於
抗日份子等不遑之徒予以
嚴辦不稍寬貸倘有此種
莠民匪居速告發以免
玉石俱焚為要
日本軍指揮官

war poster of the Japanese army

The soldier is wearing a kind and gentle expression. On his left is a Nanjing man holding something in his hand. He is bowing and totally submissive to the soldier. On the right is a woman of Nanjing in a kneeling position with a small pot in her hand, as if she is offering food to the soldier or receiving food from him. The caption suggests the latter to be the case.

We should not easily be taken in by the lies of enemies. During the fall of Nanjing, there were many stories of brave and tenacious resistance against the aggressors. We, however, must also admit that under

Zhonghua Gate was decorated with the slogan "Building a new order in East Asia," an order dictated by Japan.

This picture shows two huge characters meaning "peace," at a time when Nanjing had been occupied for two years by the Japanese invaders.

the enemy butcher, many residents in Nanjing succumbed. On walls brought half way down by Japanese bombs were huge characters of "peace" and on the tower of Hanzhong Gate were the words of "Building a new order in East Asia." It was impossible to expect everyone to unswervingly join the resistance. History goes by page by page. We should not only

The once renowned Central University is now the infantry hospital for the Japanese forces.

Wang Jingwei swearing in his puppet regime

In April 1941,
Nanjing was the site of
a celebration marking
the "return of the
capital" by Wang
Jingwei's puppet
regime.

The mayor of the renegade Nanjing government reviewing young scouts

recognize part of it nor should we easily let go of some of the fragments with too much generosity. After the incident of September 18, 1931, Wang Jingwei angrily resigned from his post in the Nationalist government in protest of Chiang Kai-shek's policy of non-resistance. At the time, his enthusiasm for resisting Japan was high. And in the early days of the war of resistance, he spoke loudest in advocating a scorched earth policy so as to leave nothing for Japan. But he was the very person who later became China's arch

The "National corps" doing physical exercises. The word "national" only made people turn red with shame, for China was already under Japanese occupation.

renegade, as he closely cooperated with Japan.

I could not hide my shock when I saw these pictures for the first time. Scouts were drilling and girl students in skirts were doing "National corps" exercises. Fully armed soldiers were blowing bugles. Such scenes were only too familiar. When the war broke out, the streets in Nanjing were permeated with the spirit of military resistance and scenes like these were everywhere. More alarmingly, the original caption for the picture with blue sky and white clouds as the background was "Youth of new China on the march." Here the expression "new China" referred to Nanjing under the renegade government of Wang Jingwei. In these photos, the blood had not yet been wiped from the

The original caption of the picture says "Youth of new China on the march."

The model of the bomb is no longer seen at Xinjiekou Square. In its place is a slogan extolling Wang Jingwei, known for being an eloquent speaker. Before the breakout of the war of resistance against Japan, his speeches were exemplary articles read by many students.

streets, houses destroyed had not been rebuilt, and women once raped still had flames of hatred burning in their hearts. And yet the loss of memory was already clearly evident in the scenes in Nanjing at the time. History mercilessly left its record of those who surrendered to Japan. This they could not deny.

The Xinjiekou Square that used to have the huge bomb now had a huge slogan, disgustingly extolling Wang Jingwei in these words: "Wang Jingwei is the supreme leader for rejuvenating China." The renegades should even remember the word "rejuvenating," which they used as a cover to hide their treasonous conduct! On the entrance of the Central Department Store, there was also a slogan, saying "Congratulating our friendly ally on conquering Burma," after the Japanese army occupied this neighboring country. The slogan only laid bare the true features of the Wang Jingwei government in accepting the enemy as a friend and fawning on their masters.

On March 30, 1941, the renegade government under Wang Jingwei even had the audacity to hold a massive military parade and an "exhibition of documents on peacefully building the country." They did not want to resist the invaders but had the nerve to sing the tune of peace. If the

The Central Department Store. On both sides of the entrance are slogans congratulating Japanese troops for conquering Burma.

following two pictures are paired together, viewers will surely find them disheartening. One shows a woman who still carries a trace of a scar after being sexually bullied. Another shows a health contest for babies born soon after the war broke out. The war was still being waged but all was already forgotten.

What Nanjing should congratulate it self for was that toward the end of World War II, the city did not suffer the bombing of allied forces. The city once incurred great disaster because of its resistance to aggression, then became part of the Nazi camp, declaring war on

A "healthy boy," winner of a contest held during the Japanese occupation

Refugees at the refugee camp of the College of Humanities at
Jinling Girls University

A healthy children contest during war time

A singing contest publicizing the "peace movement"

The Confucian Temple after Nanjing fell under Japanese occupation. A close look reveals many Japanese soldiers.

the allied troops. Now, without firing one shot, it suddenly became a victor. After the surrender of the Japanese forces, joyful Nanjing residents poured onto the streets. This reminds one of the words Chiang Kai-shek wrote after the incident of September 18, 1931, around the time he wrote the blank check of resistance. He said in effect that he knew he was no match for Japan. And so his fighting did not mean winning over Japan but only protecting national dignity. This was a cunning argument. And the trend of development of the war of resistance against Japan partly proved what he said to be right. In battle after battle the Nationalist army under his command was defeated. Defeated as they were, they never surrendered. As long as there was a gasp of air, they would continue to resist Japan. Then, in the end, the international situation changed. Japan was defeated and China emerged as one of the victorious "big four powers." Of course, to describe China as one of the "big four powers" was self-

Learning that Japan had surrendered, residents of Nanjing rush to the streets to celebrate.

The background of this picture is apparently not Nanjing. The purpose of the picture is to brag that China had emerged as one of the big four powers at the end of World War II.

Commander-in-chief of the Nationalist army He Yingqin arrives in Nanjing to accept the Japanese surrender.

People erected an archway to welcome the return of the Nationalist government to Nanjing.

Returning to Nanjing eight years later, Chiang Kai-shek seems a bit embarrassed.

aggrandizing. Before World War II ended, Chiang Kai-shek proposed to Churchill, with a smile, that he would want to recover Hong Kong and Kowloon from Japan. Churchill's reply was short and crisp: "You will have Hong Kong only over my dead body."

I find it really hard to imagine how Chiang Kai-shek could hide his embarrassment. Where was his personal dignity and where was the dignity of the country? As far as the war against Japan was concerned, we have to admit that to a certain extent we won without much fighting. The people of Nanjing, though they suffered unprecedented destruction and endured the hardships of war, did not triumph over Japanese invaders militarily. When the war was over, the forces that had led to the military failures of the Nationalist troops did not go away. And the shadows weighing on the heart of residents in Nanjing still existed.

As a victorious army, the Nationalist troops later

built a "booty museum" on the hill slope where the Wutaishan Gymnasium stands today to display captured enemy's cannons, guns, and war planes. Though the museum was meant to celebrate a victory in the war, the captions on the display items were so meticulously worded that they did not have the tone of a victor. Victory came too suddenly and was somewhat hard to explain. It seemed that people in Nanjing did not rest on the laurels with a clean conscience. Yet to be sure Nanjing did pay a heavy price for the war and the price not only included the killing, burning and looting the city incurred, but also the huge submission people endured during the years of Japanese occupation. And this submission meant humiliation of the spirit and soul, which was no less hard to bear than

Entering the government office, Chiang has regained his confidence.

抗战胜利的象征。

The booty museum to display the spoils of victory over Japan

the physical massacre. Like the massacre, it was a wound deep in the heart of the city. Past experience, if not forgotten, is a guide to the future. Perhaps the people in Nanjing should not only remember their past humiliation but also their shame and remorse.

The original words on the picture remind people not to forget their humiliation and suffering.

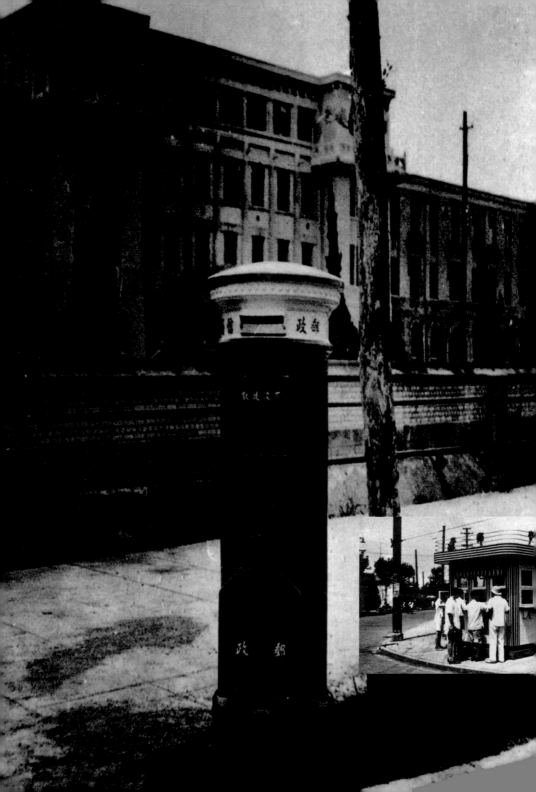

The Value
of Letters

兆言：你廿二日写的信和照片，今天上午才收到，大概是写好了没有就投邮的缘故。你爸爸到了之后就寄信给你，来信里没有说起，或者是你写信时尚未收到。你妈妈来了之后，有些日子的下午精々有些不舒服，一般说来还是好。已经托人(买车票)，说的是下月三日的十三次车。至早是十日午后到，也可能拖后一两天。拿到车票需弄通知你。三张葡萄花照片，很好，我要放在本子里。带来给我看的你爸妈的照片，我看过了，也不错。你自己也很满意，这是严格要求，我很欣赏。还有，你样々离自己搞，这神精神我尤其●欣赏。准备作一首诗给你。何日作成说不定。

神●
至十月廿六日午

This is a letter my Grandpa wrote to me in the 1970s. At the time I did not think it was necessary to save letters like this. As a result, most of the letters he wrote were lost.

For a long time during the Cultural Revolution, from 1966 to 1976, father did not exchange letters with grandpa in Beijing. Father was a "rightist" and his difficult position in the Cultural Revolution was not hard to imagine. Grandpa who was far away in Beijing was extremely worried about his son. Once he mentioned to my cousin in a sorrowful tone: "I suspect your uncle no longer lives in this world!" At the time, many people could not endure the humiliation and chose to commit suicide. Among Grandpa's friends, quite a number took the road of killing themselves, persons such as Lao She and Fu Lei, both great men of letters. Grandpa kept writing to my father but did not receive any reply. No

The earliest post office in Nanjing, taken in 1912

wonder he was thinking of the worst thing that could happen.

Later Father explained why he did not write back, and the reason was simple. At the time he was being detained and all his letters had to be delivered through his captors. Normally an easy-going person, Father became very stubborn because he thought it was a great humiliation to have his letters delivered by his captors. So he decided not to write any letters. In his later years, Father often laughed at himself and regretted his absurd stubbornness. As he advanced in age, he became more appreciative of Grandpa's eagerness and longing for his letters. Grandpa, however, never criticized Father for what he had done, but simply let bygones be bygones.

Toward the end of the Cultural Revolution, I spent a year living with my Grandpa and his greatest satisfaction with me was that I became his mailman. It was a lonely time, as eighty percent of the family members had gone to work in the countryside in different parts of China. Writing letters became his great consolation. Everyday he expected some letters to arrive and he replied to every one of them. When he finished writing a letter, he would always ask me to get on my bike and take the letter to the mailbox standing at the entrance to the lane where we lived. Transportation at that time was not as convenient as it is today. Though they lived in the same city, Grandpa often kept contact with his old friends by letters. Each time I went to the post office, I would buy a large quantity of stamps, arousing curious looks from the sales clerk.

The role of letters is declining these days. In fact, many of us are now too lazy to write letters. I, for one, write with a computer and do not even have a pen under my roof. The popularity of telephones has quickened the process of information exchange. Now a more fashionable thing is to communicate through email. Letters are becoming cultural relics. Often I hear people say they have letters my Grandpa wrote or they have seen some in other people's homes. They are all beautifully handwritten with a Chinese brush. They suggest that the letters should be included in the collection of my Grandpa's writings. There are even people who offer high prices to buy the letters Grandpa wrote to me. Who knows, perhaps one of his hand-written letters may crop up in an antique market somewhere.

The importance of letters in the history of China goes without saying. Without mentioning those written in distant history, it is sufficient to cite the example of the wife of the mayor of Nanjing. After the Nationalist government was established in Nanjing, Ma Chaojun served the longest among the majors. His wife Shen Huilian was an active socialite in Nanjing for many

The rather fat Ma Junchao, long-time mayor of Nanjing, was a native of Guangdong. His wife Shen Huilian was also from Guangdong and was also rather fat. In this picture she is seen delivering a report.

Mailman who delivered letters in rural areas in the early 1910s

years, known as a strong woman. Before she became the wife of the mayor, she was a primary school teacher in rural Guangdong. A primary school teacher in the countryside was considered a learned person and in her case also a new type of woman. In her spare-time, she often wrote letters for illiterate rural women. Many men in this Guangdong village were working in Southeast Asia. One young wife suspected her husband was having an affair for he had not returned home for several years. So she asked Shen Huilian to write a letter on her behalf, in which she wanted to strongly scold her husband.

This young village woman could not read or write. All she asked was that Shen faithfully relay her anger at her husband. She was a very pretty woman and her anger moved Shen, who was still single at the time. Instead of scolding the man, Shen wrote a moving love letter. When the husband received it, he was truly moved by what his wife was presented as saying. Immediately he gathered his things and returned home. Delighted with the result, the young wife went immediately to thank Shen Huilian.

Before education became available to most people, many could not read or write. Ghostwriters became professionals. Outside a post office in the past, there was always a small table topped with paper, pens, or writing brushes with a man wearing glasses sitting behind it. His job was to write letters for other people. It is hard now to find out exactly how much a ghost-written letter cost at that time. The length of letters varied and the ghostwriter was always a scholarly-looking person who by nature and tradition would not openly advertise his price. A friend told me that he knew a ghostwriter who charged only ten cents for each letter. Out of this the ghostwriter would have to spend eight cents for the stamp. When the cost of the paper and envelope were deducted, he made at most just one cent per letter. This which took place in the 1950s sounds almost incredible today.

What has left a strong impression on me was the old man writing letters for others outside the post office at the Confucian Temple. During my childhood, the home of our family's maid was on the Qinhuai River bank. She often took me with her to her home to have a quick look at her young daughter. Each time, we had to pass by the post office and I always saw the old man, thin and with disorderly hair, sitting at a corner. He always seemed rather lonely. In my experience, I never saw anybody ask

A man who tried to make a living by ghostwriting letters for others

A mailman from the Nanjing Lingyuan Post Office delivering mail

him to write a letter. More and more people were able to read and write and the ghostwriting of letters as a profession was obviously soon to disappear. It was a great pity for men who could write to meet such a fate.

In the old society, only children of well-to-do families had the money to go to school. There were many chances open to them. To be in such a sorrowful state as to have to live by writing letters for others was by no means a successful career.

There is an old saying that when you move a tree, it may die, but when a man moves to another place, he

The picture, taken in 1947 by the Public Service Section of the Post Bureau, shows a mailman doing house delivery of letters.

will have new chances. In the past those who were open-minded and daring left their homes to look for opportunities elsewhere. When they got old, they returned to their hometown, just like weathered leaves falling to the ground. Letters served as the bond between them and their families while they were away from home.

A postal service advertisement of 1948

Postal service was quite advanced in ancient China. During the Han Dynasty, from 206 BC to AD 220, a view of the postal service of a given place would reveal the degree of economic development there. The book *Han Office and Old Practices* says that "Every five *li* (one *li* equals half a kilometer) there is a post office with a mailman in the middle. Each way he only had to travel half the distance." The volume on Xue Xuan of *The Book of Han* recorded that when a man named Xue Xuan passed by Chenliu, a small county seat, he discovered that the bridges and post offices were in poor conditions, which led him to conclude that there was something wrong with the administration of the county.

The ancient tradition of paying particular attention to the postal service remained unchanged up to contemporary times. There were official post stations for transporting government documents while there were post offices serving the public. During the reign of Emperor Guangxu (1875-1908) of Qing, the government had a ministry of the post and the job of the minister was similar to that of the minister of communications. In essence, "post" here means communication. A study of China's postal history, therefore, is a study of the history of communications in the country.

China's modern postal service began with the efforts of foreigners, just as was the case in other communication areas. Over a century ago, the imperialist powers set up many post offices. The volume on communications in *Manuscripts of the Qing Dynasty* records there were 9 British, 14 French, 14 German, 16 Japanese and 5 Russian post offices in China. The United States lagged behind, having only one. These post offices were operated by foreigners and were not confined to the coastal foreign concessions, but extended to cover inland areas as well. The presence of these post offices objectively provided great convenience to smuggling, for the Chinese government had

The poster indicates that some of the post offices in Nanjing were open 24 hours.

no jurisdiction over them and could not look into the operations of these foreign-operated enterprises.

Postal service during the Republican period (1919-49) was fairly advanced. As the national capital, Nanjing naturally boasted the best postal facilities in the country. The Nationalist government gave particular attention to its postal services. On New Year's Day in 1912, the Nationalist government was established at Nanjing and Sun sen was sworn in as the

A postal flag in 1919

A publicity window on Taiping Road shows the changes and improvements of mail delivering tools.

provisional president. He immediately appointed Tang Shouqian to be the post master. An old bureaucrat, Tang took the job not because he really wanted to do anything, but because he liked the fame accorded by the title. Soon after he took the office, he went to enjoy an easy life in a foreign concession in Shanghai. His 34-year-old deputy, Yu Youren, became the real administrator. A revolutionary, Yu immediately rectified the postal service once he took the job. He decided to issue a commemorative stamp to replace the Qing Dynasty stamps. He dispatched a departmental director, Chen Tingji, to the Commercial Press in Shanghai to print 1,200 new stamps.

Mailmen leaving the post office on Taiping Road for delivering mail on their motorbikes

Before the new stamps were printed, the postal service had to continue with the older stamps. A measure taken to accommodate the situation was to put a chop with the words of "Republic of China" on the Qing Dynasty stamps for continued circulation. A senior official in the postal ministry of the Qing government was a Frenchman. To brag neutrality, he put a chop announcing "temporary neutrality" on the Qing stamps for public sale. As there was a huge storage of the Qing stamps, they quickly occupied the market. So there was a strange situation in which there were three types of former Qing stamps in circulation at the same time. The first two bore the words of either "Republic of China" or "temporary neutrality." The most absurd was the third that carried both chops whose characters were printed on top of each other. Yu believed this situation was the result of the foreigners' attempt to split the Republic and detrimental to the unity of the Republic of China. He issued a message to the nation to get rid of these stamps, or he would not continue to serve as deputy postmaster.

To judge whether or not the postal services were advanced, you have to see the scale of the business. As early as in the late Qing period, the newly established Nanjing Post Bureau gradually eased out the private post offices. For some time, private post of-

Three kinds of stamps circulating simultaneously

fices had been quite popular in Nanjing as they were found on big streets and in small lanes. In 1934, there were still seventeen such places, but they were already finding it hard to continue to operate as their business was declining. The government-run post bureau in Nanjing, however, grew quickly in size. At the beginning, it operated from a rented small room with a monthly rent of only twenty yuan. Most of the private offices did not think much of the post bureau while residents of the city mostly maintained a wait-and-see

Bicycle-riding
mailmen ready to set
out for delivery

Staff of Jiangsu
Post Administration
taking mail to Xiaguan
Railway Station

Motor tricycles for
mail delivery

固程利使金储 立 局政邮
其图挽附府匯局 二 政邮

局業匯金儲政郵京南

THE POSTAL REMITTANCES & SAVINGS BANK. NANKING.

The facade of the Postal Remittances and Savings Bank, Nanjing

An office for postal savings service. The service was introduced in 1919 and the interest rate was 4.5 percent. In 1922, the interest rate was cut to 3.6 percent.

A postal service vehicle used in 1991 by the Nanjing Post Bureau

Maqun Branch Post Office

Nanjing Lingyuan Post Office

A postal box on Shanxi Road, Nanjing

A postal service pavilion in Nanjing

A new style postal
service pavilion at the
Confucian Temple

attitude. Later the residents discovered that the government post bureau delivered mail faster and cheaper than could the private post offices. Besides the government ones did not charge "liquor tips, " which was a bad practice that the private post offices maintained. In the early days well-to-do families did not mind giving tips, but as mail exchanges became more frequent among the common folk, people became careful about what they spent and they soon discovered the advantages of the government-run postal service.

In 1899, Nanjing became a trading port and the post bureau was put under the administration of the customs office. At the beginning, the post bureau simply served Nanjing, but four years later it expanded its business scope to all of Jiangsu Province and further on to other parts of the country. At the time there was no railway service and all mail had to be delivered by mail-

The young woman is putting a letter into a mailbox. This photo is from an album on fashions.

men on foot or by boat. In 1912, the Jiangsu Post Bureau spent 250,000 yuan to build a three-story office. Later a spacious sub-bureau was built on Gongyuan Street. In the 1930s, there were fourteen post offices of fairly large size and scale that mostly still operate today.

Post offices were quite wealthy institutions and

Mobile auto post offices may seem strange today. Here is the first mobile auto post office with an old-fashioned vehicle, in March 1947.

People could get into the mobile auto post office to do business.

At this mobile auto post office, most visitors were women. Perhaps women in the past had a deeper interest in letters.

postal officials were much over-paid. It was a good fortune if a young man could find a job in a post office. The office buildings of the Railway Ministry and Communication Ministry were certainly first-class. The building of the Communication Ministry was constructed as an office building for the Ministry of Post and Telecommunications with funds earmarked for postal services. The post bureau actually occupied one-fifth of the south wing of the building of the Communication Ministry. The size of the building of the ministry proved how adequate was the funding for postal services. The building in Sajiawan, now occupied by the Political Science Institute of the People's Liberation Army, was designed by Yang Tingbao and was completed in 1933, on an area of 115,000 square meters. The building had a surrounding wall protected by a moat. In front of the building were flower beds, a garden, and a creek with small bridges. Inside was a complete system of central heating, carpets, and leather chairs. There was also a huge ballroom decorated with colourful wall lamps, chandeliers, and murals.

Since the postal service was not short of money, sponging from it was naturally commonplace. In 1916, the service showed a surplus every year, but under the impact of the incident of September 18, 1931, when Japanese aggressors took the three northeastern provinces, funding for the preparations for war increased with each passing day and funds for the postal service were often diverted to subsidize China Airlines, despite the complaints of the postal administration. Postal service was a government business and, as such, benefited as well as suffered from being so. The channel for the postal business to make money was its "postal savings service." According to statistics of

1935, there were 700 offices handling "postal savings" with 200,000 clients making deposits. The total sum deposited amounted to more than 50 million yuan. With such a business, the postal service certainly had things to brag and boast about. After the victory over Japanese aggression, the postal service in Nanjing once again quickly developed. Unfortunately the government resorted to the same methods in managing its money, using money from the postal service for other emergency use, thus in the end bankrupting the postal service.

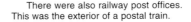

There were also railway post offices.
This was the exterior of a postal train.

Interior of a railway post office, taken in 1948

Prominent Residences in the Republic

Portrait of Chen
Sanli in his late years

Chen Yan'ge with his
wife and daughter

In 1900 a prominent scholar, Chen Sanli, moved his family to Nanjing. Being a great poet of the late Qing Dynasty period, he was known as the "poet of poets." As the saying goes "like father, like son," his children were also outstanding. Chen Hengge, his eldest son, was a painter who was the teacher of Qi Baishi, one of the greatest painters in the 20th century. Chen Yan'ge, another son, caused people to raise their thumbs in respect whenever his name was mentioned. When the Reform Movement of 1885 that was initiated by bourgeois reformists failed, Chen Sanli was condemned "never to be appointed again to any position" because of his sympathy for the reformists. Thus Chen Sanli moved his home away from the capital city of

Chiang Kai-shek's
villa at Tangshan Hill

Beijing to Nanjing and stayed away from politics. After that, he lived for thirty years in Nanjing. His old residence was on the First Lane of Xihua Gate. Naturally it was a large house surrounded by a big garden.

In the early 20th century, many traditions were still obvious in Nanjing. Distant from the political center, wealthy, prosperous and packed with men of letters, this was a city fit for people in cultural circles. There were occasions of war to be sure. The Taiping rebels came in a rush and perished in a hurry. Then the Hunan army rolled over with all its might. Chaos only added more vicissitudes to life. Over its long history, every now and then, Nanjing would endure a period of war. There was the Revolution of 1911, the restoration of the Beiyang (Northern) warlord regime, and finally the most brutal invasion by Japanese aggressors. People in Nanjing acquired a particularly quick adaptability to heal from the wounds of war and regain their vitality for life.

Nanjing is a most appropriate place for generating stories of history. In 1927, the Nationalist army took Nanjing and made it their capital. Interestingly, despite his meritorious performance in battle, Chiang Kai-shek, who had just gained national power, had to resign. While away from the political center, Chiang did not waste his time. He used it to launch a hot pursuit of Soong May-ling. In war affairs, Chiang was a victor, but in politics he suffered setbacks. Now he needed to beef up his confidence and strength through love. He needed a woman who could help him. Soong May-ling had gone to study in the United States at the age of nine. And his marriage to such a Westernized woman resulted in Chiang's pro-US stand later on.

"Meiling Palace" was a short form of the name of this building: Residence of the Chairman of the Nanjing Military Commission.

Chiang Kai-shek seemed to love this building on the campus of the Nationalist Central Military Academy. Historical documents often mention the name of the place, Qilu.

Chiang brought his bride to Nanjing. Zhang Jingjiang, a Nationalist party veteran, refurbished his villa at the Tangshan Hill and offered it as a wedding gift to Chiang and his new wife. The building looked rather ordinary from the outside with reddish brown bricks and tiles. The wall was built with stones quarried from the hill. In appearance, the two-storied structure seemed to be just a one-storied house. You found its charm only when you went inside. This suburban villa was particularly noted for its basement that was as luxurious as a Turkish royal bath. Tangshan Hill is famous for its hot springs and was naturally an ideal site to build luxurious villas.

During the days when Nanjing was the capital of the Republic of China, Tangshan Hill was a resort for high-ranking officials of the ruling Nationalist party. The very names of the villas told of the pretensions of their noble owners. Dai Jitao's villa was named "Cloud Viewing Study" and Yu Youren's, "Millet Thatched Hut." Chiang's villa at the hill certainly set an example for villa building by the upper class in Nanjing. One after another, villas sprang up as the number of private houses owned by officials quickly increased. On Sundays, people could often see the white-bearded Lin Sen, president of the country, and Wu Zhihui, a party veteran known for his sense of humor, in the shaded streets or on small roads on Tangshan Hill.

The Republican period was a time for massive construction in Nanjing. Old bureaucrats and new nobility all flocked into this city and it began to change. Such changes, however, never got out of hand. Nanjing was a city with a sound culture. The new opportunities were not going to change the aesthetic traditions of the city over night. In this city, being flashy and without substance would not get a man anywhere. Nor would someone without learning achieve anything. The

A bird's eye view of Wutanshan (Wutai Hill)

city did not like the rough and uncultured upstarts. Small buildings emerged like mushrooms after a spring rain, each obtaining its own individuality. If you take a

walk along Yihe Road today, you will discover that the owners of the houses half a century ago must have been men of learning, culture, and varied tastes. Among the residences of the bureaucrats, no two looked exactly the same. Instead, they showed a myriad range of architectural features. Even those belonging to the same architectural style carried some variations. Those built with a European architectural style were divided into Northern and Southern European features. And those of Northern European traditions manifested styles popular in different years of Northern Europe.

A new residential district in Nanjing, located at today's Yihe and Xikang roads

Murphy, born in 1877, was a well-known American architecture designer. Lu Yanzhi, the Chinese designer who designed the Sun Yat-sen Mausoleum, was his assistant. Responding to an invitation in 1928 to advise on the construction in the capital city, he completed the Plans for the Capital, the first document of standard construction planning for Nanjing.

Blueprint for the Nationalist government done by Murphy

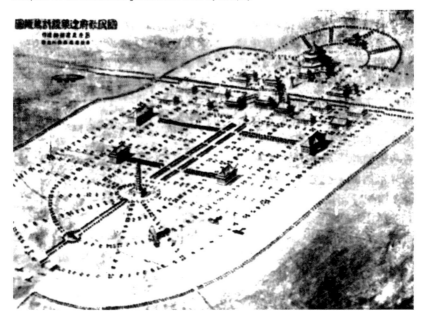

If outstanding teachers and students of architectural design were lucky enough to be in Nanjing during that period: they could bring their talents into full
play. Among such were Lu Yanzhi, designer of the Sun
Yat-sen Mausoleum, and Yang Tingbao, designer of
the auditorium of Central University and the radio
station. In the 1930s, many architects and designers
came to Nanjing to demonstrate their skills and
knowledge. The world was then going through a

A plan for urban
construction in Nanjing
by Lu Yanzhi

depression. So long as someone had money, he would find it easy to hire people of ability to work for him. Nanjing had become a stage for designers and architects to vie with each other.

The residences of the new bureaucrats could be seen just about everywhere in Nanjing. The house of T.V. Soong stood on the Beijige Hill. That of Kong Xiangsi (H. H. Kung) was at Xiangpuying, those of Wang Jingwei and Yan Xishan were built on Yihe Road. The residence of Lin Sen was at Shibanqiao, those of the two brothers K. F. Chen and L. F. Chen on Changfu Street, that of Dai Jitao on Huaqiao Road, that of Li Zongren (T .J. Li) at Fuhougang, that of Bai Chongxi at Yongyuan, that of Tang Shengzhi at Baiziting, that of Zhou Fohai at Xiliuwang, that of Chen Cheng on Lingyin Road, and that of He Yingqin (Y. C. Ho) on the ground within the campus of today's Nanjing University.

I spent seven years studying at Nanjing University and every day for those seven years I passed in front of Ho's house. Today, his residence houses the foreign affairs office of the university. To be accurate, however, the foreign affairs office only occupies a part of the original residence. According to historical records, Ho's house was built in 1934, but the Ho's residence we see today was rebuilt on its original ground in the late 1940s. The original house was burned down when Nanjing fell to the Japanese.

We cannot see the original design of Ho's house, but in Nanjing today there are a large number of well-preserved official residences that date from the early Republican period. Like the residence of Ho, their occupants have changed. The very ground where Ho's house was built could be said to be a place of historical interest. It was where people for ages watched chicken fights. It is said that during the early years of the Republic, when Huiwen and Hongyu institutes were merged to create Jinling University, someone saw a huge brick carved with the characters: "Ancient Chicken Fight Ring." With the Drum Tower at the background, the spot, not far from the center of the city, was rather quiet, making it an obvious golden piece of land. When his house was being built in 1934, Ho was at the height of his career. If he wanted to

He Yingqin (Y. C. Ho) was a lucky man. He occupied a high position and lived a long life, almost a hundred years.

have a house built, he certainly could pick the best spot and the best architect.

Ho's residence occupied nearly two-thirds of a hectare of land and the architectural style was a combination of both Chinese and Western features. Consider the materials used for example. There were both traditional glazed tiles and modern steel-reinforced cement. Ho was a solider and his house had to satisfy the needs for the preparation for war. It was said that the courtyard contained an underground fortress unknown to outsiders. It is also said that soldiers of an engineering corps were brought in to destroy it in the 1950s. His residence consisted of two buildings and four one-storied houses with a total of thirty-one bays of rooms all painted in a yellowish, milky color. The courtyard was shaded by trees and embellished with flowers. There were French windows, a spacious meeting room and a series of elegantly decorated small chambers for secret meetings and talks. Many important decisions in contemporary Chinese history were made in these chambers, including those surrounding the Xian Incident. During that incident, Chiang Kai-shek was held under house arrest and officials in Nanjing went to Ho's home to find a solution. Ho took the

Luxurious houses occupied by the rich and noble in the 1920s

Entrance to the Central Stadium. During the rule of the Nationalists, many interesting buildings were erected, but unfortunately they were ruined by Japanese invaders.

position of sending military forces to Xian for he believed that "They should not care for Chiang's safety at the expense of the fate of the state." Some newspapers thus printed stories of how Soong May-ling charged into Ho's residence, scolding him for harboring his own scheme to kill Chiang Kai-shek by sending out forces to fight those who were holding Chiang captive.

A bird's eye view of the Central Stadium, large enough to accommodate 60,000 spectators. At the time, this stadium was the largest of its kind in East Asia.

Seat of the Sun Yat-sen Mausoleum Administrative Committee, destroyed during the war

Building of Ministry of Railways

This was the seat of the national government in 1927 when Chiang Kai-shek had just arrived. Its shabby look is obvious.

The presidential palace in 1948, still lacking style. Although the entrance looked simple, the inside was well furnished. Chiang Kai-shek had a hard childhood and did not want his residence to be showy. To live a plain life was a part of his "new life movement."

Ministry of Communications during the Republican period. Taken in 1935, the picture reveals the charm of the building of that period.

Entrance to the Ministry of Communications

Entrance to the Examination College, which was one of the five major institutions of the Nationalist government

The Hualin Hall of the Examination College. It was where Dai Jitao, president of the Examination College, spent his leisure time.

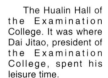

199-189 The Wenli Pavilion housed the "Tablet of Confucius Studying Rituals" and related stone carvings. The stone carvings, which dated back to more than 1,500 years, were destroyed during the Cultural Revolution.

The old Nanjing
Railway Station

Many history books treat the Xian Incident as the turning point of Ho's falling out of Chiang's favor. My view is that Ho knew nothing about commanding soldiers to fight battles. It was not that Chiang did not put him in an important position but that Chiang was simply too kind to him. Ho was a classmate of Chiang's and all his life he thrived on this relationship.

In 1930, an army commander by the name of Feng Yunting suddenly resigned from his post and came to Nanjing to engage in real estate business. Apparently he made a big fortune out of it. During the war against Japan, he fled to his hometown in Shaanxi to hide. When the war was over, he came back to Nanjing to continue his old trade. He had a long list of properties and the income from rent was huge. Many of the houses occupied by high officials of the government were rented from him. Yu Youren, the president of the supervision council, was an honest official who had no money with which to build a house. So he had to rent a place to live. Feng rented one of his houses to Yu Youren for the rate of 1.2 million yuan a month. The rented prop-

Yu Youren was famous for his long beard and beautiful calligraphy.

The old Navy Ministry

erty included a Western style building, six one-storied houses and a courtyard four-fifths of a hectare in size. The rent judged by the standards of that time was not high. It was the post-anti-Japanese war years and the economy under the management of Chiang Kai-shek and his trusted officials was deteriorating. Inflation had become so serious that the nation was on the brink of becoming bankrupt.

The period around the 1930s was the best time to invest in real estate in Nanjing. It was a time that a hundred and one things were being done at the same time. Construction was going on everywhere. "To build a new capital" was an exciting slogan of the day.

People not only built their houses where the city government prescribed, but they built them wherever their wishes took them as long as they picked a favorite spot and had the economic means to construct them. In December 1932, Xu Beihong and his wife Jiang Bihui, who had lived in a dormitory at Central University, happily moved into their new residence. Xu's house was at Fuhougang, only a few hundred meters away from where I now live. The land was originally a graveyard. As residents in Nanjing tended to live in the southern part of the city, the area north of the Drum Tower was rather desolate. After the Nationalist government made Nanjing the national capital, property soared in price. Without much money, the Xus acquired the land in the northern part of the city where prices were also soon to rise quickly, with a payment made available by Wu Zhihui. For about one-seventh of a hectare, the land cost 3,000 yuan.

After they acquired the land, they advertised in a newspaper for the owner of the graveyard to relocate the remains of the deceased. This was an age of buying land, a time when Feng Shui masters were

Jiang Bihui with Zhang Daofan. Jiang was the former wife of Xu Beihong and the lover of Zhang Daofan, a senior official of the Nationalist government. Jiang and Xu divorced each other during the war of resisting Japan.

enjoying a brisk business. What seemed absolutely normal then really sounds absurd today. Once you had a piece of land, everything that followed would be easy to arrange. If somebody came to remove the remains of the deceased, it was fine. Or, when the advertised deadline for removal was over, the land would be treated as if there were no graves.

Many of the details were attended by Xu's wife, Jiang Bihui. Xu had already established his fame as a painter by then, but he seldom managed to have his works sold. Wu Zhihui generously paid the money to buy the land, but Xu had no money to build the house. When recalling that period of their lives, his wife said that she often took their children and the housemaid to wonder about the land they had bought. This gave her a sense of happiness for she was sure a bright future was lying ahead. The house, complete with all the facilities she imagined, was more moving than the real thing. The designer's wife was a graduate from the Fine Arts Department of the university where Xu taught. So she was his student. With this relationship, the student's husband, the designer, had to do his best.

The residence of Xu Beihong, though it could not compare with those

The currency drastically devaluated and Chinese people had to take bundles of money with them when shopping.

of officials, was good enough to make others living in bad conditions admire it with envy. Besides the large patch of green grass, the magnificent entrance, the bamboo fence, and the two-storied building the fence surrounded, Xu's studio alone was suffice to surprise people. The studio was 10 meters long, 8.3 meters wide, and 5.3 meters tall. In the courtyard there were two huge poplar trees. According to one story, there were only three examples of this kind of tree in Nanjing. The third was in the southern part of Nanjing. The height of the trees makes them quite conspicuous. Since the trees were tall, one could see them while riding a train as one approached Nanjing on the Shanghai-Beijing Railway.

Chiang made a big mess of the economy. Notes of money piled up high show that Chiang's rule was coming to an end.

After the war against Japan, the price of property in Nanjing shot up. During war times, a house was just a possession, but in times of peace, the importance of a house became increasingly obvious. Those who had and those who did not have may be two totally different kinds of people. Unfortunately the period of peace in Nanjing did not last long, as war broke out once again between the Communists and Nationalists. As a result, the city's residents suffered severely from the economic crisis. People who were used to an easy life now rented out their houses to make some money to cover their everyday expenses. Only foreigners could afford to rent luxurious residences in Nanjing since they were too expensive for the local poor. A part of

Senior Nationalist government and party officials fleeing from Nanjing to Taiwan

Ho's residence, for example, was rented to the US embassy for a monthly fee of US $150. Jiang Bihui and Xu Beihong had already been divorced by that time and their house was put under her name. She rented the house to the French embassy for an annual rent of US $3,000. These signs spelt the pending downfall of Chiang Kai-shek. People knew that if they wanted to save money, they should save US dollars, for the prospect for peace was not clear. In fact, further earth-shaking changes would soon take place.

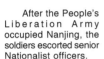

After the People's Liberation Army occupied Nanjing, the soldiers escorted senior Nationalist officers.

Scenes in Historical Anecdotes

A panoramic view of Gulin Temple. Such a nice place could only be appreciated by people with literary talent.

Knowing historical anecdotes but leaving behind no written record of them is a great pity. Mr. Hu Xiaoshi, for example, was a born and bred Nanjinger, and once enjoyed a great reputation as a professor of Central University. Another person well informed about the tales of Nanjing history was Lu Qian, also a native of the city. Had they written what they knew about Nanjing, it would have made fascinating reading.

The stone lion in front of the entrance to Gulin Temple bears a vivid facial expression.

University professors in the past often had an interest and taste in traveling as tourists. Men of learn-

A distant view of Jiming Temple (Rooster Singing Temple)

ing enjoyed the charm of culture and the waters and hills of distant places. They were imbued with culture. In December 1928, four professors at Central University went to have dinner at the Zhonghua Restaurant and then hired a vehicle to take them to the Gulin Temple on Stone Hill west of the city. After that, they crossed the Sanbu Liangqiao (Three-step and Two-bridge) and walked along the ancient Qingliang (Clear and Cool) Road, passing by the Returning Cloud Hall to arrive at a famous spot described by Mei Zengliang in his widely-read piece, "A Visit to Lesser Pangu." It must be pointed out that that "Three-step and Two-bridge" and "Clear and Cool" were real street names. Such names reveal the atmosphere of culture.

During the early Republic period, residents in Nanjing found Qingliang (Clear and Cool) Hill a good place for outings. After 1949, a crematory was built and the hill began to mean something else to the people who went there again.

For a long time, Nanjing had carried a distinctive cultural style whose aesthetic taste was closely related to its long cultural traditions. After novelist Zhang Henshui settled down in Nanjing, his study faced east toward the Purple Hill. As soon as he opened his window, there was a view of it that resembled a traditional Chinese landscape painting. It was a living scroll, changing with the four seasons and giving the viewer different impressions. No wonder whenever he put words on paper there was a piece of beautiful writing running thousands of characters.

Wanzai Pavilion at the Black Dragon Pool

Old Nanjing was like a painting to be sure, but not everyone had the feeling of living against such a scenic background. Beauty must be felt through a man's senses. Beauty is a discovery that requires the sensitivity of men's souls. Ever after the Tang Dynasty (618-907), scenic views in Nanjing could not be separated from a sense of nostalgia. The scenic beauty of Nanjing has always been related to the vicissitudes of history. In the 1930s, a tablet marking the location of Meixiang Tower was discovered near the Wuding Bridge on Dashiba Street, providing proof that Li Xiangjun, the heroine in the story *Peach Blossom Fan*, indeed once lived here.

Without what has happened in history, without the traditions of people's learning and knowledge, an ordinary-looking bridge like the Wuding would not have aroused the tremendously strong sense of nostalgia that it did. For years, whenever I see the picture

Wuchao Gate, ruins of the palace of the Ming Dynasty

The Qixia (Cloud Lingering) Hill is a famous holy site for Buddhists where statues in the grottoes are valuable cultural relics. Unfortunately, the abbot at the temple Ruo Shen hit upon a most bizarre idea and applied a layer of cement to the statues in 1923, resulting in their losing their original charm.

of the lotus-shaped pinnacle of the Baoen Temple, I am overwhelmed by a sense of melancholy. Ever after Emperor Yongle moved the capital of the Ming Dynasty to Beijing, residents in Nanjing could not shake off the feeling of being survivors of a great era. The Baoen Temple was built by Emperor Yongle in memory of his mother, who was tortured to death by the founding emperor of the Ming Dynasty soon after he was born. After Yongle took the state power from his cousin, he had the temple built in 1412. From this picture of the temple, taken in 1890, we can infer the magnificence of the original structure before it was destroyed in the flames of war.

The pagoda of the temple was more than a hundred meters tall. On its first level, was a huge horizontal tablet announcing: "The First Tower under Heaven." The pagoda was so tall that people could see its grand posture even from boats traveling on the Yangtze. The pagoda consisted of three parts, the "supporting plate," the "wheel" and the "pinnacle." The supporting plate weighed 2,250 kilograms, the wheel 1,800 grams, while the pinnacle was cast with 2,000 taels of gold. The inside of the pagoda was illuminated by 146 lamps that consumed 30 kilograms of oil every 24 hours. Soon after it was completed, the pagoda was struck by lightening. Repair work continued until it was finally destroyed during the infighting of the Heavenly Peace troops.

The Baoen Temple was located outside Jubaopen Gate, south of the city proper. The area of the southern suburbs has always been a tourist resort with Oxen

Head Hill, where General Yue Fei of the Southern Song Dynasty fought bravely against the northern invading troops of Kin, and the tomb of a king from ancient Brunei, a foreign monarch who died of illness on a visit to China in 1408. Traditionally, tourism in China was inseparable from tomb sites. In the southern

The pinnacle of the pagoda at Baoen Temple. Without an explanation, people may view it as a water container.

suburbs, there is also the tomb of Fang Xiaoru, a noted scholar, who was asked by Emperor Yongle, after he had taken over power from his cousin, to write an announcement of his ascent to the throne. Dressed in funeral garments, Fang wrote one character meaning "power usurping." Emperor Yongle then told him: "This is a private matter within my family and you have no right to say anything." Fang swore at the emperor who was enraged and shouted: "Aren't you afraid of having all your relatives punished for what you have done?" "Not at all!" was Fang's reply. As a result, the emperor had all the Fangs, men and women, young and old, put to death. Still Fang Xiaoru was not going to give up, so his teachers and friends were also punished. In all, several hundred people were killed.

People in Nanjing seemed to highly appreciate the kind of gallantry demonstrated by Fang Xiaoru. But bravery meant invitation to death. As a result, all those who survived became submissive, having suffered many humiliations. To be brave, one had to be idealistic. In the classic novel, *The Scholar*, there are two Nanjingers who survived by working as carriers of human manure for fertilizing the fields. After they sold the manure every day, they would go to the Yongning Spring Teahouse to have tea. Then they went to the Rain and Flower Terrace to watch the sunset. Their behavior moved Du

The tomb of Fang Xiaoru. According to historical records, when all his kinsmen were killed one by one, he did not give up but simply shouted at the killers.

Shenqing, the hero of the novel, who said with a smile, "It is true even for these most ordinary citizens; one can detect the traditions of the past when Nanjing was the imperial capital!" This story is a most vivid description of the easy manner of the people in Nanjing.

It was an obviously enjoyable thing to watch the sunset on the Rain and Flower Terrace, which commanded the highest point in the southern part of Nanjing and had always been a strategic place. In recent centuries, its strategic importance increased with the introduction of guns and cannons. During the Revolution of 1911, a fierce battle was fought here between the revolutionaries and the Qing troops. During the War of Resistance Against Japanese Aggression, the "battle to defend Nanjing" also saw a tug of war here. For years, the terrace had been a place where people went to remember the dead as they were accustomed to burying their deceased ones on mountain slopes.

A stone tablet in the southern suburbs in 1890

The Rain and Flower Terrace held a strategic position. This picture was taken in 1890.

There, during the Bright and Clear Festival (an occasion to remember the dead in spring), whole families would come out to visit the tombs, go to the teahouse, and then have a good meal at Maxiangxing Moslem Food Restaurant.

It was after Nanjing became the capital of the Republic when the eastern suburb became a busy scenic tourist spot. With the completion of the Sun Yat-sen Mausoleum, the people in Nanjing, and in fact all over the country, suddenly found a new place worth

Yongning Spring Teahouse. Lu You, a 12th century poet, described the spring as the second best in south China. The place is mentioned many times in the Qing Dynasty classic novel, The Scholar.

visiting. For people from outside, whether or not one had been to the mausoleum became a measurement of having been to Nanjing. There was the Xiaoling Mausoleum of the Ming Emperor, but it was a royal cemetery. It was a crime punishable by death for people to venture into it without authorization. Consequently, common folks stayed away from visiting the final resting place of the Ming emperor. After the Qing Dynasty replaced the Ming, the royal mausoleum fell into desolation, as it was poorly maintained. Unless someone had a special interest, they would not go to the eastern suburbs. Those who visited the tomb in private were usually people with lofty ideals, harboring anti-Qing plots and plans to restore the Ming. They did not go to the mausoleum because of its scenery.

The Xiaoling Mausoleum of the Ming Dynasty in 1865. What else can best express the desolation of history!

The Sacred Path leading to the Xiaoling Mausoleum of the Ming Dynasty, 1890

Visitors to the Xiaoling Mausoleum in 1900

丁未十月桂辛京卿樣舟白下鈺與多泰太守約謁明陵題過商品陳列兩持攝景以志斯游即呈桂辛京卿鑒存鴻鈺題記

At the invitation of Duan Fang, viceroy of Anhui, Jiangsu, and Jiangxi provinces, Zhu Qiling, an official of the 4th rank, came from Beijing in the winter of 1909 for a visit to Nanjing. The man on the left is Zhu Qiling on a visit to the Xiaoling Mausoleum.

Old Nanjing·Reflections of Scenes on the Qinhuai River ⊙ 219

A soldier at the Xiaoling Mausoleum

An open tea stand at the Xiaoling Mausoleum

Monument of War Martyrs, also known as the Linggu Pagoda, is now a major scenic site of the Purple Hill Scenic Area.

The Sun Yat-sen Mausoleum made the eastern suburbs a place for people to remember him and express their lofty aspirations. Up to this day it is a place where primary and secondary school pupils receive education on patriotism. People go there with a sense of esteem for the democratic revolutionary. Because of the emergence of the Sun Yat-sen Mausoleum, the Ming emperor's mausoleum also seems to have gained vitality. The founding emperor of the Ming Dynasty, who had been dead for more than six hundred years, benefited from Sun Yat-sen. Actually at the Sun Yat-sen Mausoleum, the Nationalist government built a series of complementing projects including cemeteries for martyrs who died in establishing the Republic of China. The nine-storied, sixty-meter tall Linggu Pagoda, as a monument dedicated to the memory of these martyrs may seem somewhat lower than the pagoda of the Baoen Temple, but it is high enough to serve its

Archway at the War Martyrs Cemetery

purpose. I remember visiting Linggu Park when I was in primary school. We climbed to the top story and pushed off folded-paper and watched them dance in the air. It was a great fun!

The war martyrs' monument, Sun Yat-sen Mausoleum, and Ming emperor's tomb are three important sites in the eastern suburbs. People come to see the suburban scenery but also to get a sense of the burial culture of China. The monument to the war martyrs was designed by Murphy from the United States and one has to admit he was a smart man. When he designed the Jinling Girls University in 1925, he was not familiar with traditional Chinese architecture. The buildings thus did not look nice. Moreover, the bracket under the roof's eave was off-line and did not correspond to the top of the pillar. Now, built merely three

A corner of the War Martyrs Cemetery. In the lower part of the picture are the tombs and standing at the back is Linggu Pagoda. Hidden in the woods is a memorial hall housing the tablets of the martyrs.

"Monument to War Martyrs of the Songhu Battle of the Fifth Army." The Fifth Army was under the direct control of Chiang Kai-shek and its commander was Zhang Zhizhong. Among the 128 martyrs selected by drawing lots for burial here, 50 were from the Fifth Army. During the battle of August 13, 1937, this army had fought bravely against Japan and the man who directed the fight was Zhang Zhizhong.

years later, the monument in traditional architectural style which he took pains to design easily gained the approval of the captious committee.

The cemeteries did not go against traditions for building mausoleums. From the picture, we can see that the three cemeteries form a rather obtuse triangle, leaving a large space for the lawn. Meanwhile, the design took into consideration a combination of old and new structures by cleverly turning the old beamless hall into a memorial service venue, through adding creative ideas to traditional structures. What strikes people is the crisscrossing network of small paths in the first cemetery. Some one thousand tombs spread out along the paths, revealing a sense of homely warmth in a solemn atmosphere and a human flavor in the general mood of bravery. The cemetery was completed in 1932, soon after the January 28 Songhu Battle in Shanghai. The government selected by random lot drawing 128 martyrs (to coincide with the date of January 28) to be buried in the first cemetery as a way of expressing their determination to fight Japan. To encourage the living by remembering the dead is after all an international practice.

Although described as the capital of kings and emperors, Nanjing, since its recorded history, has generated more stories of passions of love and sorrow

Kuixing Pavilion

than gallantry. There was no short supply of emperors who saw the demise of their kingdoms, a fate that the Chiang Kai-shek ruling clique did not escape. Chiang's purpose in proposing "Living a new life and forbidding opium smoking, gambling, and prostitution" was to put an end to the dejected and dispirited history of Nanjing. People here did not only live in the shadows of the lamps and the sound of oars on the boats of the Qinhuai River during the first half of the 20th century, they lived in an atmosphere of war. When the country was in difficulty, it was every citizen's job to defend it. The mausoleums in the eastern suburbs should have encouraged people in their patriotic conduct.

When I was still a child, the southern part of the city was much more lively than the northern part. When people went to Xuanwu Lake Park, they normally took a bus, going through Jiefang Gate and getting off at the Jiming (Rooster Singing) Stop. The first thing that greeted their eyes was the Kuixing Pavilion. I did not like the shape of the pavilion to begin with, but detested it more when I grew older and learned that it was a memorial built by the Wang Jingwei renegade regime in 1941 to mark the occasion when Nanjing became their capital.

Not far from the pavilion is the Ancient Rouge Well. When the Sui army fought its way into Nanjing, the last emperor of the Six Dynasties who ruled from 583 to 589 jumped into the well together with his beloved concubine, in an attempt to commit suicide. But they did not die and were captured alive. Unfortunately, all the crimes associated with the demise of the dynasty were heaped upon the concubine who was killed instantly. What suffered most during the war, however, was the city of Nanjing which was burned down by the

The Ancient Rouge Well, site of a story of the "woman disaster"

Sui army. Emperor Wen of the Sui, who reigned from 581 to 604, ordered that the city be totally burned and demolished so that it would no longer exist. No wonder poems written about the city in later dynasties always carried a sense of sorrow at the mention of Nanjing.

Beyond the Ancient Rouge Well is Xuanwu Lake where the park has long been the pride of Nanjing people. Before the breakout of the war against Japan, it

The 1930s was the prime time of the Republic. Girl students are pictured here on an outing. There were so many places to visit in Nanjing at the time.

The ABC Ice Cream Store near the Confucian Temple

Restaurants in the 1930s looked more or less the same as those today.

was a place people felt deeply attracted to. Nanjing is a very hot city and the lake provides a good summer resort. Before air conditioning was available, the rich and noble would go to Mount Lushan in the neighboring province to escape the summer heat. Xuanwu Lake Park would open its gates to the public free of charge. People would leisurely walk in the park, waving fans in their hands and finding a favorite spot to sit down for a nice chat. Or they might hire a boat, rowed by a boat woman, to enjoy a cruise on the lake. Summer activities at Xuanwu Lake Park were once a miniature form of the prosperity in Nanjing.

Literary works about Nanjing would not end without a mention of the boat women, apart from dealing with the singing girls on the Qinhuai River. Beautiful and young, the boat women made many men's heart beat faster. In the park, there were not only pink peach blossoms and green willow trees, there were also other trees like cherry, crabapple, magnolia, and others one could name. In fact the lakeside was another place, besides the Qinhuai River, for romantic affairs. *The Morning Post* of April 10, 1937 had this report under the headline "Rascals Running Rampant on Xuanwu Lake:" "The authorities are urged to take measures to tackle rascals, now that it is turning warm and the peaches are blossoming on Xuanwu Lake. People in the city, including young women, all want to go for a visit as long as they can find the time. The entrance has seen a steady stream of vehicles and visitors. As people come to enjoy the site, rascals be-

Cherries in the early part of the 20th century cultivated at Xuanwu Lake were known far and wide. A local fruit from Nanjing, cherries were often mentioned in ancient poems.

A bird's eye view of Xuanwu Lake

Summer on Xuanwu Lake

gin their evil doing. They chase decent women in the name of rowing boats on the lake. Such lake rascals greatly disturb tourists. It is hoped that the security authorities will attend to the matter."

The old Nanjing has been long gone, but its history is not to be forgotten. In the early 1930s, Zhu Qi returned to China after doing his doctoral studies in Germany and became a young professor and chair of the Department of Economics of Central University.

Mr. Zhu, deeply attached to the scenery in Nanjing, was not only good at writing about it but also took many fantastic pictures. At the time he came to Nanjing the city was experiencing massive construction by the Nationalist government as roads were being paved, houses rebuilt, and places renamed. Everyday the city changed its physical look. Ancient sites were being abandoned and ruins destroyed at an unprecedented rate. Mr. Zhu spent three years taking more than two thousand pictures in order to let people who came afterwards have a sense of history, since they could not see the real things. His works *A Collection of Historical and Scenic Sites in Jinling*, *An Illustrated Study of Ancient Sites in Jinling*, and *An Illustrated Study of the Mausoleums from the Six Dynasties* have become valuable documents presenting scenes in the years that have gone by. It is because of these pictures that many historical tales about the city can be told and people allowed to once again submerge themselves in the lost scenes.

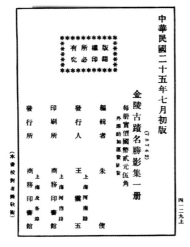

The copyright page of the 1936 edition of A Collection of Historical and Scenic Sites in Jinling. The author of the book left us with many historically valuable pictures of old Nanjing.

Family Picture Albums

Longpan Lake during the Republic period. These houses provided shelter to those Nanjing residents whose life had no worries.

When friends heard that I was writing about old Nanjing, they provided me with many clues. One even brought me a huge photo of their family wrapped up with a piece of outdated newspaper. Pointing to the people in the picture taken more than seventy years ago, he told me who they were: his mother, uncle....

Looking at the yellowish picture, listening to my friend's story, I could not help but think of how many people could tell interesting stories by pointing to the people in old photos. The little girl in this photo, mother of my friend, is now an old lady in her eighties. Apparently, she must have told many people who were the ones in this photo and what had happened to them, one by one. Perhaps she first told the story to young

A family photo taken in the 1940s

A family photo taken in 1920, courtesy of a friend of mine

A mother with her
two kids

Such family photos
can be found almost in
every household.

friends of her age, then to visiting adults, and finally to people younger than she.

Just imagine how interesting it would be for a bride to introduce old photos like this to her bridegroom. Then they would have children and the young girl in the photo would become a mother. As she would tell the stories about the photo, her tone would change into that of a kind mother. Still later she would become a grand-mother and then great grandmother. She would keep telling stories about the people in the photo, which would bring back memories of the past, again and again.

Walls in living rooms in the past always had framed photos and many people liked to hang up pictures of the entire family. Nothing was more reflective of the

A business sign of a photography studio

Another photo of a mother with her kids. Without the family planning program, the young mother might still have several more kids.

In this photo taken in the 1930s the people must have been men of position.

The man in the middle in the front row seems to be K. F. Chen, a veteran Kuomintang official. Photos like this were assets to be shown off.

harmony and flourishing of a family than a photo with every member in it. Normally people would pick an auspicious day to take such a photo, such as the birthday of an elder in the family or the day when a youngster returned from studies abroad. From the very beginning a whole family photo was commemorative.

A similar picture would be a photo of a given collective. A family photo, as a window to the family, told viewers the style and mood of the family, while a collective photo reflected socialization and demonstrated one's social position and cultural background. It would offer an insight to one's experience and a certain stage of life. Many col-

In November 1936, the Nationalist government arrested seven people, condemning them for "sabotaging the Republic." Shen Junru, a leader of the national salvation association of all walks of life, and the six others were actually calling for an end to the civil war and a campaign to resist Japanese aggression. The event came to be known as the "Seven-gentleman Incident." After their release, they had this photo taken with Ma Xiangbo, a veteran patriotic figure in Nanjing.

A student publicity team of the 1930s

lective photos were destined to possess great historical significance. Aesthetically, collective photos always
had the drawback of everyone in the photo being too
serious and stiff. Compared with family photos, collective ones lacked a human touch. There were many opportunities for collective photos, such as cornerstone
laying ceremonies or the completion of a building, college graduations, and a conference or a meeting of
VIPs. Among those in a collective photo, there would
always be some
who became better
off and provided
the subject for
talk. To have a
photo with public
figures was thus a
lucky thing.

Once a collec-
tive photo had
been taken, it
would be dupli-
cated in many
copies for the safe-

A free medical
consultation photo
taken in Nanjing in the
1940s

keeping of each person. A collective photo was an important symbol of one's position. For the rich and noble,
photo taking was a time to be patronizing. The more
prominent a person was, the more collective photos he
would appear in. Meanwhile, collective photos were
often used as proofs of one's past glory. Many people
liked to hang up their graduation picture and photos
with public figures in the most conspicuous spot of
their home. Such collective photos often became part
of the interior design of one's homes.

From collective photos, the viewer can obtain a

sense of the trend in history. For example, a photo of "free medical consultation" taken in the 1940s is an interesting one. There are many people in it and the muscles on every face seem rather tense. In fact, the entire hospital is in the picture from the registration office to the surgical department, from the internal medicine department to the acupuncture department, and from the doctors to the patients. You name it, and you will find it on the photo. On the pillars is a couplet. The first sentence announces "Doing kind things and not seeking a false reputation." The reflection of the light makes it impossible to read the second line.

Another example is the "children in scouts outfits" taken in 1947 in Nanjing. As I can imagine, these kids appear to be refugees as they have no shoes and show a trace of worry on their faces. Had their parents

Look at the expressions of the children, one by one, on this photo taken in 1947

General Zhang Xueliang and T. V. Soong on a boat ride on Xuanwu Lake. Apparently the photo was taken before the breakout of the War of Resistance Against Japanese Aggression. The two of them had been long-time friends. After the Xian Incident of 1936, Zhang was tried in a military tribunal and then for a long time held under house arrest at Soong's home.

Girl students on an outing in the 1930s

Girls outdoors in the 1930s. I imagine this photo was likely to have been taken by a man showering special attention on the girls.

been alive, they would have had a happier childhood and would not have looked at the camera with such sad eyes.

College girls in the 1940s. They wore their school badges. Somehow they do not seem as innocent as those in the 1930s.

Among the old photos, the ones that reveal easy expressions are those taken when people went on outings. At the time, cameras were not as popularly available as they are today. When people went out, there were not many opportunities to have photos taken. Those interested in photographing were then often regarded as people who neglected their duties and were interested only in playing. As young women loved having their photos taken, knowledge of how to take photos gave young men one more means of attracting women. Once I heard a story in which a returned student from Germany professed that he had studied medicine in Germany and advertised himself as being well-versed in both Chinese and Western

A family going on an outing

medicine. His family used to operate a pharmacy. Not a skilled doctor, however, he eventually had to close his clinic. Instead, he opened a photographic studio. Being a womanizer, he would take photos for young women free of charge. In the end, his studio lost money.

When I was in middle school, the Cultural Revolution was in its late stage. Students did not have to do serious studies and we actually did what we liked. I often went to plays with a friend several years older. At the time he was working as an electrician, living in a dilapidated room of about six to seven square meters in a corner of a large courtyard. I happened to be interested in fixing radios, and when I had questions or lacked spare parts, I would visit him. A lonely person, he was not interested in making friends. Perhaps he thought I was younger and therefore knew less than he did. He regarded me as his bosom friend, often telling me what was on his mind.

The box containing his mother's ashes stood on his dining table. Each time I visited him, I felt uneasy. I could not understand why he kept the box there. From childhood, I was afraid of dead people. Whenever I saw a funeral procession when I was on the way to school, I would quickly take a detour. My friend realized my fear and put the box under his bed in front of me. Still I felt somewhat uncomfortable, feeling there was something still existing where the box used to stand. On the wall was

An outdoor photo

Singer Zhou Xiaoyan performing for the first time in Nanjing

his mother's picture when she was young. The photo was taken when she was in the university. She had a hairdo like that of actresses from Hollywood and looked pure, healthy and elegant. Her eyes were bright, penetrating every corner in the room. No matter where I stood, as long I looked up, I saw her lively eyes. I could never link up the pretty young lady in the photo with the ashes in the box, now wrapped up with a piece

Painter Fu Baoshi had this photo taken by the Xuanwu Lake before he went to study in Japan.

of red cloth under the bed. The beautiful young woman in the picture and the dilapidated room were in sharp contrast. The pretty eyes that bespoke of tenderness and love watched every person who looked at her photo. Her lips revealed a mysterious smile, like that of Mona Lisa.

Learning that I had become a writer, my friend would tell me stories about his mother. Born into a family of wealth and class, she brought a large patch of houses to her new family as her wedding dowry. Later all the houses were confiscated and she and her son had to squeeze in a makeshift room in the compound once she owned. Many old photos show that the times have changed. Her boyfriend was an officer in the Nationalist army, loved photography, and often took his fiancee to the suburbs.

Photos taken in studios always show their subjects to be stiff and yet interesting.

The background of this studio photo was too fake.

The young officer took many pictures of his girl friend. Later they got married and went to a studio to take their wedding photo. He later went to the battlefield and then she received a notice of his martyrdom. How he died was not known.

She eventually married a tricyclist and gave birth to her only son who was my friend. It was a marriage without love and the couple often quarreled. In the end they were divorced. Moving away from her second husband, she devoted all her love to her son. For a long time, the old photos were her only consolation. Later, she became mentally unsteady. One day she flew into a rage without reason and burned all the old photos. After being struck ill with something not very serious, she soon died. After her death, my friend went to the house of an old friend of her mothers, borrowed a small-size photo, and had it enlarged at a studio. It was that photo that I saw on the wall.

Among family albums, almost every old yellowish photo has a story behind it. Some of the stories are about twists and turns in life, while others are rather dull. As time goes on, however, they acquire new meanings. There are many stories associated with old photos. When I was in secondary school, naughty students often made fun of an old lady living in a house that was on our way to school. They threw small stones into her house and, if they

People can guess whether they were sisters or friends.

heard something being hit and smashed into pieces, they would run away.

Almost every student who had walked along that street knew the story of the old lady, a kind of story people liked to tell. When young, she was a singing girl on the Qinhuai River. She was very pretty at the time, as proved by a photo hanging on her wall. An enlarged photo, in a wooden frame, faced the window on the side of the street. People walking by invariably would slow down and take a look. The photo had artificial colors, accentuating her pretty features, red lips, white teeth and thin eyebrows, which gave her every look of a sexy girl. Too young to understand things, we could not really comprehend what being a singing girl meant. So we referred to her as a female secret agent, because we had seen a movie in which the enemy secret agent was as pretty as she was.

Stories about the old lady, like flying birds, seemed to have wings and traveled quickly. People naturally gossiped, saying how she behaved when she was young.

I don't remember when she died; neither can I remember when I began to grasp the full meaning of the term singing girl. All I remember is that she lived a lonely life by herself.

Finally the old lady's story evaporated from this street. Once I dreamed of walking on the road I used to travel on the way to school. When I woke up, what I felt was most surprising. I had dreamed of that artificially colored photo facing the window in the house by the street.

Old photos in people's homes are windows to history. Through these windows, we can review the distant past and look ahead to the future. Futures cannot be detached from the past. What has gone by will

This photo was taken in the 1920s. It is hard to believe that it was as early as that.

This lady has a mysterious smile.

inevitably become intimate reflections. I love to look at old photos that have so much history in them. Some seemingly casual focuses of history will become valuable only when that history cannot be repeated.

For many old photos, words to describe them seem too weak and helpless. Many of the explanations are unnecessary. People in the photos will forever exist, recording the instances of years in the past and these instances will be eternal.

Such a broad and hearty smile was apparently not intended just to impress people.

Editors' Note

Changes a city has undergone are an important part of the history of the development of a civilization. In publishing this series of books, we have been guided by one consideration, i.e., to give readers a brief history of some well-known Chinese cities by looking at some old sepia photos taken there and reading some remembrances with regard to those cities.

Not like conventional publications, each book of this series contains a large number of old photos selected to form a pictorial commentary on the text. This provides a good possibility for readers to learn about Chinese urban history, cultural evolution in urban society in a new perspective. It also enables readers to re-experience historical "vicissitudes" of those cities and relish feelings of urban folks of China in the modern times.

To better illustrate those cities, we have commissioned renowned writers who have not only lived in their respective cities for a long time but also have been known for their strong local writing style. Either in presenting a panoramic view of a city or depicting fate of men in street, their writings are always so natural yet full of feelings.

This series of books have been published originally in Chinese by Jiangsu Fine Art Publishing House. The English edition has been published jointly by the Foreign Languages Press and Jiangsu Fine Art Publishing House.

Foreign Languages Press
October 2000 Beijing

图书在版编目（CIP）数据

老南京：旧影秦淮／叶兆言著．－北京：外文出版社，2002.10
（老城市系列）
ISBN 978-7-119-03048-7
I.老...　II.叶...　III.南京市－地方史－史料－英文　IV.K295.31-64

中国版本图书馆CIP数据核字（2002）第023408号

中文原版

选题策划	叶兆言　何兆兴　顾华明　速　加
主　　编	朱成梁
副 主 编	郭必强
著　　文	叶兆言
图片供稿	中国第二历史档案馆
	夏奕藩　高建中　纪　峻
	蔡涌波　顾华明　张修文
责任编辑	速　加

英文版

策划编辑	兰佩瑾
翻　　译	黄　玲　郝　薇
英文编辑	卓柯达
责任编辑	兰佩瑾

老南京·旧影秦淮

© 外文出版社
外文出版社出版
（中国北京百万庄大街24号）
邮政编码：100037
外文出版社网址：http://www.flp.com.cn
外文出版社电子邮件信箱：　info@flp.com.cn
　　　　　　　　　　　　　sales@flp.com.cn
深圳市佳信达印务有限公司印刷
中国国际图书贸易总公司发行
2003年(大32开)第1版
2009年12月第1版第2次印刷
（英汉）
ISBN 978-7-119-03048-7
08000(精)

老城市

OLD CITY